KARANIS
REVEALED

KARANIS REVEALED

Discovering the Past and Present of a Michigan Excavation in Egypt

Edited by
T. G. Wilfong

With the assistance of
Andrew W. S. Ferrara

Kelsey Museum Publication 7

Ann Arbor, Michigan, 2014

In memory of Traianos Gagos (1960–2010)

Image Sources
Sources for figure images are given in captions; object photographs are Kelsey Museum file photographs, except for the following:
Randal Stegmeyer for the Kelsey Museum: **2**, **8**, **17**, **28**, **29**, **30**, **32**, **49**, **74**, **76**, **79**, **81**, **88**, **124**; Andrew T. Wilburn: **135**

Cover
Foreground: Statue of a seated priest (KM inv. 8218, number **1** in the catalogue)
Background: Image by artist John Kannenberg, derived from photographs he took on a visit to Karanis in 2010. The image is based on a view of Lake Qarun (Moëris in Greek, Mer-wer in Egyptian). The center of the Fayum farming region of which Karanis was a part, the lake featured in ancient Egyptian myths as a site of creation. This graphic was originally created to accompany Kannenberg's *Mer-wer Remix Project* based on a field recording made in the lake itself (see pp. 179–181 for a description of this project).

Published by
Kelsey Museum of Archaeology
434 South State Street
Ann Arbor, Michigan 48109-1390
http://www.lsa.umich.edu/kelsey/research/publications

ISBN 978-0-9741873-9-6

Contents

Preface

In 2011 and 2012, I curated a two-part exhibition at the Kelsey Museum of Archaeology called "Karanis Revealed," devoted to the findings of the 1924–1935 University of Michigan archaeological field project in Egypt at the site of Kom Aushim, modern Karanis, and related sites. Michigan's excavations at Karanis, a Graeco-Roman period townsite in the Fayum region, yielded tens of thousands of artifacts and thousands of archival photographs and records documenting the excavation. The exhibition was initially conceived of as an installation of archival photographs and documents, a complement to the author's 2012 article in the *Oxford Handbook of Roman Egypt*, which used such material to examine the practices and processes through which the Michigan team carried out and recorded its excavations at Karanis. The founder of the Kelsey Museum collections, Francis Kelsey, considered the documentation of the excavation of the site to be of equal importance to the artifacts the site yielded, and this emphasis on recording findings and processes generated a substantial body of records. The rich archival material for the Karanis expedition in the Kelsey Museum documents not only the findings of the excavation itself but also the context of the excavation in the 1920s and 1930s, recording the project's complex history at the University of Michigan as well as its place in the world of western archaeological projects in a transitional time in Egypt's history.

As the exhibition developed, it quickly became clear that the original plan of focusing solely on archival material would tell only part of the story of the Michigan Karanis expedition. The extensive collection of artifacts from Karanis in Ann Arbor, ceded to the University of Michigan by the Egyptian government in a generous division of finds, is so rich and varied that it seemed impossible to mount any exhibition on the Michigan Karanis project without including artifacts. And the overall conception of the exhibition was broadened to include a wide selection of these artifacts, including papyri from the excavation now kept in the University of Michigan Library's Papyrology Collection. Although Karanis artifacts routinely appear in Kelsey Museum special exhibitions and in the museum's permanent installation, a thorough overview has only been on display once, in Elaine K. Gazda's landmark 1983 exhibition, "Karanis: An Egyptian Town in Roman Times," which used the entire exhibition space of the Kelsey Museum and the publication for which remains the standard introduction to the site. The space available for "Karanis Revealed" was much more limited, so its survey of artifactual material had to be more selective, focusing on significant groups of objects to illustrate specific aspects of the history and culture of Karanis and its excavation.

As preparations for the two installations of the exhibition progressed, it became clear that a significant part of the story of the Michigan Karanis expedition lay in the current and ongoing research on the material it yielded by curators, faculty, staff, and students from the University of Michigan. Such projects include new work on known artifacts and papyri, the discovery or rediscovery of important unpublished artifacts and archival sources, new field research at Karanis, and even sonic investigations of the site and its history. All of this work came to inform the exhibition and to shape the course of its publication. Initially, the idea was to publish a modest exhibition catalogue consisting primarily of a checklist of objects and archival material on display, but this confluence of new research suggested a less traditional publication—less of an exhibition catalogue and more of a an overview of the exhibition and a presentation of the new research that informed it.

Introduction

Karanis was one of the many towns and villages founded in Egypt in the wake of Ptolemy II's ambitious project to reclaim agricultural land in the Egyptian Fayum region. From its beginnings in the mid-3rd century BC, Karanis grew into a prosperous agricultural community in the Ptolemaic and Roman periods, not particularly exceptional for the Fayum region, where many such villages existed and thrived. Securely dated documents from Karanis break off in the mid-5th century AD, which has traditionally been identified as the point at which Karanis was abandoned. The archaeological evidence and documents from other sites, however, suggest that habitation continued at Karanis through the 5th and 6th centuries, perhaps even into the 7th century AD. Karanis was almost certainly abandoned by the 8th century AD; the remains of the town fell into ruin and were covered by sand. The site, eventually called Kom Aushim in Arabic, lay uninhabited and largely undisturbed, with small settlements growing up nearby. It was not until the later 19th century that the site of Karanis, in common with many of the abandoned communities of the Fayum, was significantly disturbed, thanks both to increasing demand for antiquities and papyri by European tourists and scholars and to the growing use of decaying ancient mudbrick, known as *sebakh*, for fertilizer in Egypt. Papyri from Karanis began appearing on the market, alerting scholars to the existence of the site, even as the *sebakh* diggers made particularly heavy inroads into the ancient town center, destroying a substantial portion of the town's more important structures.

Controlled archaeological excavations at Kom Aushim were first undertaken by Bernard Grenfell and David Hogarth for the Egypt Exploration Fund in 1895, as part of their wider survey of the Egyptian Fayum region. The excavators and their sponsors were primarily interested in papyri and, beyond confirming the identity of the modern Kom Aushim with ancient Karanis, found little of interest at the site. They concluded that the site was largely looted and would be unrewarding for further investigation. The subsequent appearance of substantial quantities of papyri from Karanis on the antiquities market in the early 1920s suggested otherwise, however, and ultimately led the University of Michigan to begin a new project at the site.

ARCHIVES

Archival materials—photographs, maps, plans, drawings, notes, memoranda, records, and motion picture footage—document the activities and findings of the University of Michigan Karanis excavations and form an essential starting point for research. The following articles survey archival sources for the Karanis excavations and provide an example of the kinds of research the archives can inspire and inform.

Karanis in the Kelsey Museum Archives

Sebastián Encina

In 1923, Francis W. Kelsey was able to secure funding from University of Michigan president Marion Leroy Burton to create the Near Eastern Research Fund for explorations in Africa and Asia. From the $50,000 fund, $15,000 was budgeted for excavation and exploration in Egypt (fig. 1).[1] These funds laid the foundation for Michigan's excavations at Karanis, which would eventually become the cornerstone of the Kelsey Museum of Archaeology's collection.

The archives at the University of Michigan, at both the Bentley Historical Library and the Kelsey Museum, now house the records created from the excavations at Karanis. This collection offers scholars interested in the Karanis excavations a treasure trove of information. Spread between the two repositories, the Karanis archives support the collections at the Kelsey Museum by documenting the work performed in Egypt and provide provenance for the artifacts stored at Michigan and in Egypt.

Researchers routinely use this material to make sense of the site, to note the distribution of artifacts, and to study life in Roman Egypt. Current excavators study the archives to know what has been discovered there previously and where at the site excavations were conducted. These researchers, and others, can look through the 19 boxes of archives at the Kelsey and roughly 200 boxes at the Bentley, which contain letters, lists, drawings, reports, journals, and indices. There are also maps of the site and elevations, to go along with more than 6,500 photographs of Karanis (in addition to 705 photographs from Dimé, 639 from Terenouthis, and 444 of the Fayum area in general) (fig. 2). And we are fortunate to have 23 reels of motion picture film taken during the excavations. The combinations of items from the archives help educate students and scholars and paint a richer picture of the 68,438 artifacts discovered at Karanis (46,514 held at the Kelsey).

But the archives do much more than fill in the story about the objects and the archaeology of Karanis. As crucial as that is, the materials held by the University of Michigan also offer glimpses of other important events taking place in the 1920s and 1930s. Hidden in plain sight within the papers, letters, and film researchers

[1] F. W. Kelsey to M. L. Burton, 25 September 1923, box 64, folder 7, Francis W. Kelsey papers, Bentley Historical Library, University of Michigan.

Fig. 1. Page one of Francis Kelsey's proposal for funding field projects in Egypt and the Near East, 25 September 1923 (courtesy Bentley Historical Library, University of Michigan).

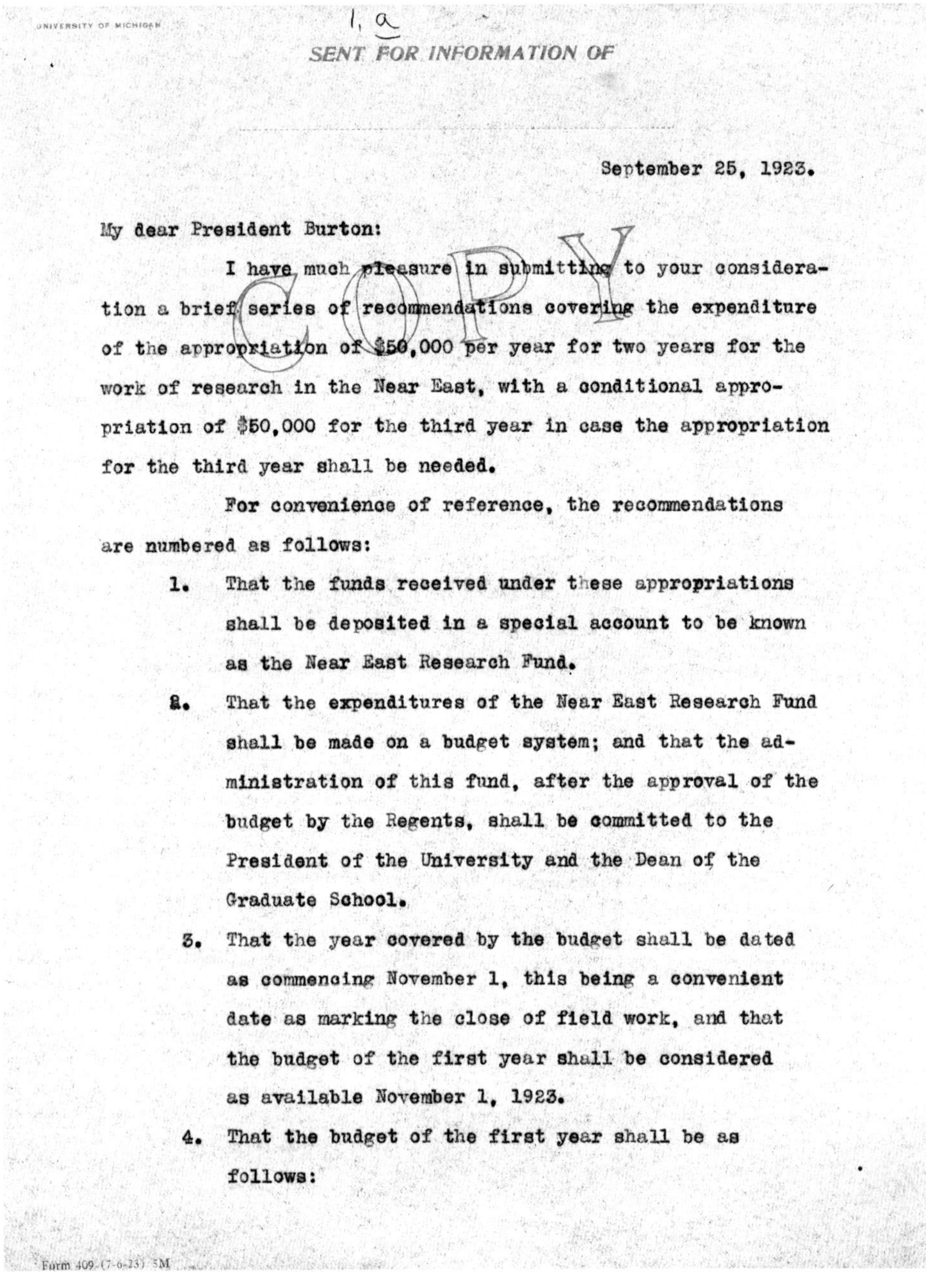

UNIVERSITY OF MICHIGAN

1, a

SENT FOR INFORMATION OF

September 25, 1923.

My dear President Burton:

I have much pleasure in submitting to your consideration a brief series of recommendations covering the expenditure of the appropriation of $50,000 per year for two years for the work of research in the Near East, with a conditional appropriation of $50,000 for the third year in case the appropriation for the third year shall be needed.

For convenience of reference, the recommendations are numbered as follows:

1. That the funds received under these appropriations shall be deposited in a special account to be known as the Near East Research Fund.
2. That the expenditures of the Near East Research Fund shall be made on a budget system; and that the administration of this fund, after the approval of the budget by the Regents, shall be committed to the President of the University and the Dean of the Graduate School.
3. That the year covered by the budget shall be dated as commencing November 1, this being a convenient date as marking the close of field work, and that the budget of the first year shall be considered as available November 1, 1923.
4. That the budget of the first year shall be as follows:

Form 409 (7-6-23) 5M

Fig. 2. View of Karanis during the excavations, looking west over granary C123 (Kelsey Museum neg. no. 7.2368).

will find evidence of working conditions in Egypt. They will read about the state of archaeological practices in the early 20th century. And they will gain insight into daily life among the staff and workers.

The archives show that the excavations at Karanis were carefully planned, down to the rules and regulations for staff. Francis Kelsey was aware of the University of Michigan's image overseas and concerned about how the staff represented it at all times. Thus, the Karanis staff was bound by the University of Michigan Excavation Camps Regulations.[2] This policy had only four regulations: a staff member must always be present with workmen when work is being performed; each week must include one day of rest free from all ordinary duties (normally Sundays, except in areas where another day is customary); the use of liquors, wines, or beers is prohibited; and any discussion of religion or politics must be avoided. The need for these policies does not come without just cause, as previous explorations had resulted in uncomfortable situations for staff and workers. Kelsey moved preemptively to avoid such situations in the future.

Documents deeper within the archives tell of other matters related to Karanis but not necessarily occurring in Egypt. President Burton gave Kelsey a truck and

[2] Memorandum 14, box 2, Francis W. Kelsey papers, Bentley Historical Library, University of Michigan.

Fig. 3. Karanis house staff, photograph by George R. Swain (Kelsey Museum neg. no. 7.2370).

car to be used for overseas explorations. While in Rome, Edwin L. Swain, son of site photographer George R. Swain, was driving the sedan and accidentally ran over a middle-aged woman. Though she appeared to be unhurt at the time, she later complained of being bed-ridden and wanted compensation from the Americans.[3] Such mishaps would never make it into any site publication, but they serve as a reminder that the archives document life outside the excavations.

Besides the paper documents in the archives, the photographs also show that life in Karanis was not just about excavations. In addition to photographs of objects *in situ*, and the very important Division Album photographs depicting the split of artifacts between Egypt and Michigan, other photographs document the non-archaeological world of Karanis. Common among the collections are photographs of the Egyptian workers, not just the American staff (fig. 3). We see workers performing archaeological duties but also building the camp house (fig. 4), building a railway for removal of excavation debris (fig. 5), repairing a break in the canal (fig. 6), fixing the roof of the camp house. Servants work with the women of the site doing laundry. In their down time, workers are seen fencing, the children wait to be paid (fig. 7; a letter from Enoch Peterson dated the day after the photograph was

[3] Memorandum 15, box 2, Francis W. Kelsey papers, Bentley Historical Library, University of Michigan.

Fig. 4. The Karanis dig house (Kelsey Museum neg. no. GL00506).

Fig. 5. Building a railway for the removal of *sebakh* from the site (Kelsey Museum neg. no. 5.2466).

taken describes how he laid off 270 child workers).[4] When a visitor arrived, native dancers performed for him. A snake charmer is seen mesmerizing a snake (that snake charmer later died from a cobra bite; see fig. 8).

[4] Enoch E. Peterson to F. W. Kelsey, 28 February 1927, box 4, folder 19, Francis W. Kelsey papers, Bentley Historical Library, University of Michigan.

Fig. 6. Scene at the canal when the south bank broke: repair work, 24 December 1925 (Kelsey Museum neg. no. 655).

Fig. 7. Paying the children of Karanis (Kelsey Museum neg. no. 442).

Fig. 8. Snake charmer visits the Karanis dig house (Kelsey Museum neg. no. 653).

Fig. 9. Michigan excavators Terentieff and Haatvedt along with Plupy the dog, at the Karanis camp house (Kelsey Museum neg. no. 464).

Guests at the site were not limited to humans. The photography collection introduces the viewer to the animals who called Karanis home as well (fig. 9). Plupy the dog is seen in a mill. Gyp (dog) chases Topsy (cat). Sipsy and other unnamed cats who lived at the site were allowed to enter the camp house to hunt for mice. A donkey helped provide water for the workers.

The film reels afford the modern researcher insights similar to the photographs. They show both the archaeological business and non-archaeological activity. The camera pans over the site, showing the excavations in progress as the town is uncovered. Workers are shown carrying baskets full of sand away, while the *sebakhin* take their soil. One clip captures the process of surveying, another a Roman temple. Workers are shown uncovering, then crating, and finally packing a statue onto a camel. Other workers keep busy building or making bricks.

Meanwhile, life continues as the work progresses. A wedding procession is filmed. The camp house is shown. The servants are working (fig. 10), sometimes doing laundry or typing and filing in the office. The snake charmer makes a cameo, still alive. Camels are in the field, while a horse race takes place. A primitive Ferris wheel is seen. A shepherd tends his flock, and the camera gets a close up of a white donkey. Water buffalo, dogs, camels, cows, donkeys, and storm clouds

Fig. 10. Workers repairing a canal (Karanis motion pictures, reel Vb).

are all captured by the cameraman. A trip into the village by a Bedouin chief is recorded.

Without proper provenance and without the archives to provide documentation of that provenance, a museum artifact's scholarly value is diminished. While the objects Michigan holds are important to the study of ancient Egypt, they are made richer through the collection of maps, plans, journals, photographs, and film that document their finding. First-time researchers review this material looking for information that helps explain the artifacts, but ongoing exposure reveals more than what the excavators originally intended. The archives also show what life was like in 1920s Egypt for a group of visiting Americans and Europeans. They show what the relations were among those people, as well as between them and the indigenous Egyptians.

For the historian, the archives serve as an example of what archaeological research was like nearly one hundred years ago. Though standards for archaeological work were different then than they are currently, the levels of detail found at Karanis are still impressive. This detail is critical for the modern understanding of Karanis, and at the same time it says something about the archaeologists who were recording this information.

Since Karanis was first excavated, numerous publications have been dedicated to specific aspects of the site. Books about the pottery, topography, coins, figurines, and glass, among others, are still used by modern scholars. And much material remains for future publication. The Karanis archives offer a chance to continue working on the archaeology of the site and, at the same time, the opportunity to gain knowledge beyond excavations. When combined, the archives and artifacts work together to reveal an even greater story that is just waiting to be told.

Notes on Three Archival Sources for the Michigan Karanis Excavations: The Record of Objects Books, the Division Albums, and the "Peterson Manuscript"

T. G. Wilfong

As outlined in the previous article, the Kelsey Museum preserves a wide range of archival records and sources from the Michigan Karanis Excavations. Three sets of bound volumes kept in the Kelsey Museum Archives are particularly important resources for the excavation and its finds. Although occasionally mentioned in print, these volumes have never before been formally described. The following notes provide detailed bibliographical descriptions for these unpublished sources, in preparation for their ultimate scanning and availability as online resources.

The Record of Objects Books

11 volumes of bound typescript with annotations, titled on spines:

"Record of Objects: Karanis 1924–25: 10–82, XIV–XXI, 010–053, 100–344, 4001–4048, 5000–50096 [*sic*]" (15 + 237 + 321 pp.)
"Record of Objects: Karanis 1926: A1–AA1, B1–B75, BA1, BC38–BC77, BS1–BS42, C1 and CS1" (725 pp.)
"Record of Objects: Karanis 1927: 202–258, B101–B119" (384 pp.)
"Record of Objects: Karanis 1927: C1–C86, 1928 [*sic*] SG" Guests at the site were not limited to humans. The photography collection introduces the viewer (i + 801 pp.)
"Record of Objects: Karanis 1928: 102*–242*, B108–B172, CS23–CS130" ([i] + 821 pp.)
"Record of Objects: Karanis 1929: 116*–236*, B132–BS215, C36–CS165" (479 pp.)
"Record of Objects: Karanis 1929: D1–D31, E1–E48, F1–F59, T1–TS20, 1928 SG, 1929 SG, Y100" (631 pp.)
"Record of Objects: Karanis 1930: 132*–152*, B168–B243*, CS23–CS215, DS100–D111, E101–E112, Z100, 1930 SG" (825 pp.)
"University of Michigan Excavations: Record of Objects: Dimé I100–I115, II200–II220, III300–III305, IV401–VI [*sic*] 402; Kom Aushim 1931 S. G." (iii + 417 pp.)

"[Record of Objects: Karanis 1932–33: 199*–244*, B146–B148, CA20*–C119, C123CG[4], CS135 & CS210, SG 1932]" (279 pp.)

"Record of Objects: Season 1933–1934: Kom Aushim 158*–196*, 4007*–4041*, A601–A656, BS120–B213, BS500–B561, C74–CS210, CS400–CS425, D302; Season 1934–35: Kom Aushim 286. 288. 305; Kom Abou Billou" (699 pp.)

These eleven volumes contain a detailed listing of all finds from the Michigan excavations at Karanis, Soknopaiou Nesos, and Terenouthis. Each volume consists of detailed typescripts made in the field, subsequently bound and annotated in Ann Arbor. Paginations for individual volumes reflect actual numbers handwritten on pages, although there is considerable inconsistency as to numbering: in some volumes, rectos only are numbered, while others are numbered recto-verso. Some volumes have title pages, but most do not, so titles are supplied from the printed spines of the book.

Individual finds (consisting of single objects or bulk groups of similar objects) are listed in the Record of Objects Books by season year, structure (or area or street) where find was made, room in structure, and letters assigned to individual finds—lower case letters for pottery, upper case letters for other objects (note sample entry in fig. 11). In the cases of exceptional or unusual finds, the Record of Objects Books also record detailed findspot information, although this is not common. Information about maps or photographs of locations for finds is sometimes indicated, again most often in unusual or exceptional circumstances. This information is in the typescript made in the field, sometimes with handwritten corrections. Other handwritten notations made later in Ann Arbor provide additional information: Kelsey Museum or Cairo Museum accession numbers, photograph negative numbers, and information on dates in the case of entries for coins, papyri, and ostraka (broken pieces of pottery used for writing).

The contents of the Record of Objects books have been transcribed into an in-house database (thanks in large part to the efforts of Kelsey Museum Collections Manager Sebastián Encina and his assistants), and this database (in conjunction with the in-house collections database) allows us to compile some statistics about the excavation. A total of 68,438 individual finds at Karanis are recorded in the Record of Objects Books, finds sometimes including more than one object.[1] Of these, 38,011

[1] The totals for Dimé and Terenouthis are 1,544 and 1,757 finds respectively.

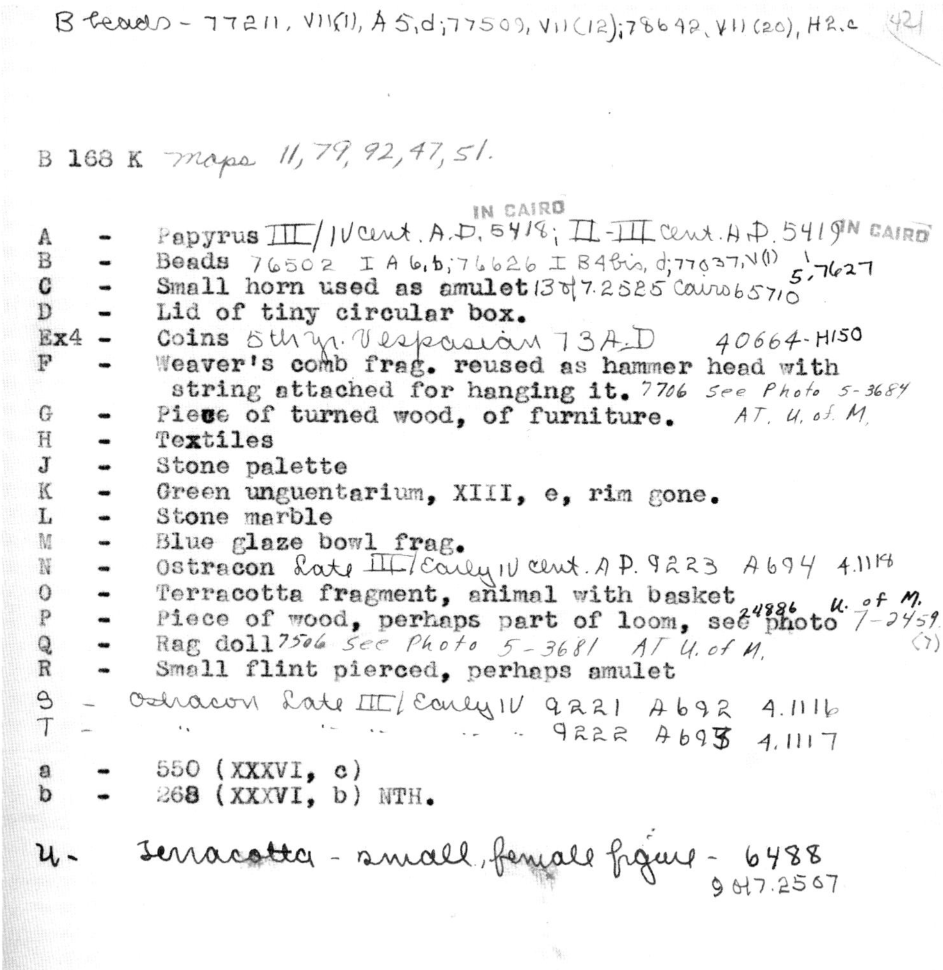
B beads - 77211, VII(1), A 5,d; 77509, VII(12); 78642, VII(20), H2,c 421

B 168 K maps 11, 79, 92, 47, 51.

IN CAIRO
A - Papyrus III/IV cent. A.D. 5418; II-III cent. A.D. 5419 IN CAIRO
B - Beads 76502 I A 6,b; 76626 I B4bis, d; 77037, V(1) 5, 76627
C - Small horn used as amulet 13017.2525 Cairo 65710
D - Lid of tiny circular box.
Ex4 - Coins 5th yr. Vespasian 73 A.D 40664-H150
F - Weaver's comb frag. reused as hammer head with string attached for hanging it. 7706 See Photo 5-3684
G - Piece of turned wood, of furniture. AT. U. of M.
H - Textiles
J - Stone palette
K - Green unguentarium, XIII, e, rim gone.
L - Stone marble
M - Blue glaze bowl frag.
N - Ostracon Late III/Early IV cent. A.D. 9223 A694 4.1118
O - Terracotta fragment, animal with basket
P - Piece of wood, perhaps part of loom, see photo 7-2459 24886 U. of M.
Q - Rag doll 7506 See Photo 5-3681 AT U. of M. (?)
R - Small flint pierced, perhaps amulet
S - Ostracon Late III/Early IV 9221 A692 4.1116
T - " " " " " 9222 A693 4.1117
a - 550 (XXXVI, c)
b - 268 (XXXVI, b) NTH.
u - Terracotta - small, female figure - 6488 9017.2507

Fig. 11. Record of Objects Book entry for structure B168, room K, 1928 season.

finds (consisting of 46,415 individually accessioned items) are in the collection of the Kelsey Museum of Archaeology, and 168 finds (consisting of 2,603 individually catalogued papyri and wax tablets)[2] are in the Papyrology Collection of the University of Michigan Library. The Egyptian Antiquities Service retained 2,462 finds and sent

[2] Note that recto and verso of individual papyri inscribed on both sides are catalogued separately, so the total of individual papyri will be somewhat lower.

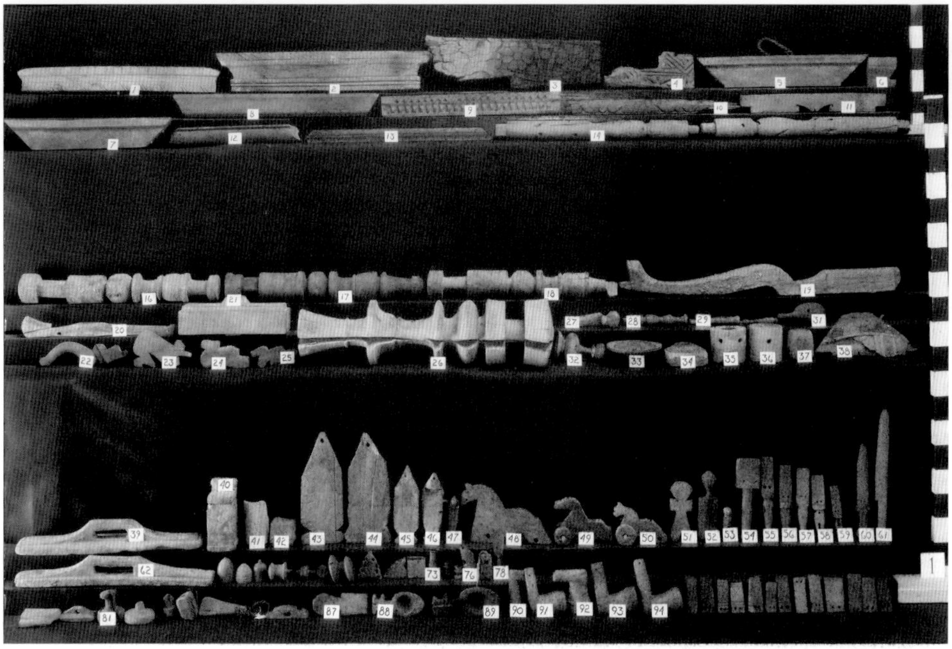

Fig. 12. Division album photograph (Kelsey Museum neg. no. 7.2513).

them to the Cairo Museum (2,101 finds), Coptic Museum (28 finds), Agricultural Museum (182 finds), and "provincial museums" in Egypt (151 finds). A total of 1,110 finds (all ostraka) were temporarily loaned to the Michigan Expedition and returned to Egypt upon publication. The disposition of the remaining 24,989 finds from the excavation is either listed as "N.T.H." ("not taken home") or left without any indication: these objects were presumably abandoned on or near the site before the division of finds since they do not appear in the division albums (for which see below).[3]

The Division Albums

Two volumes of annotated black-and-white photographs tipped onto leaves in binders:

[3] Given the nature of the objects retained by the excavators, this abandoned material must have been either extremely fragmentary or in such poor condition as to make preservation impossible. Non-diagnostic pottery sherds were not recorded in the Record of Objects Books and would have also been abandoned.

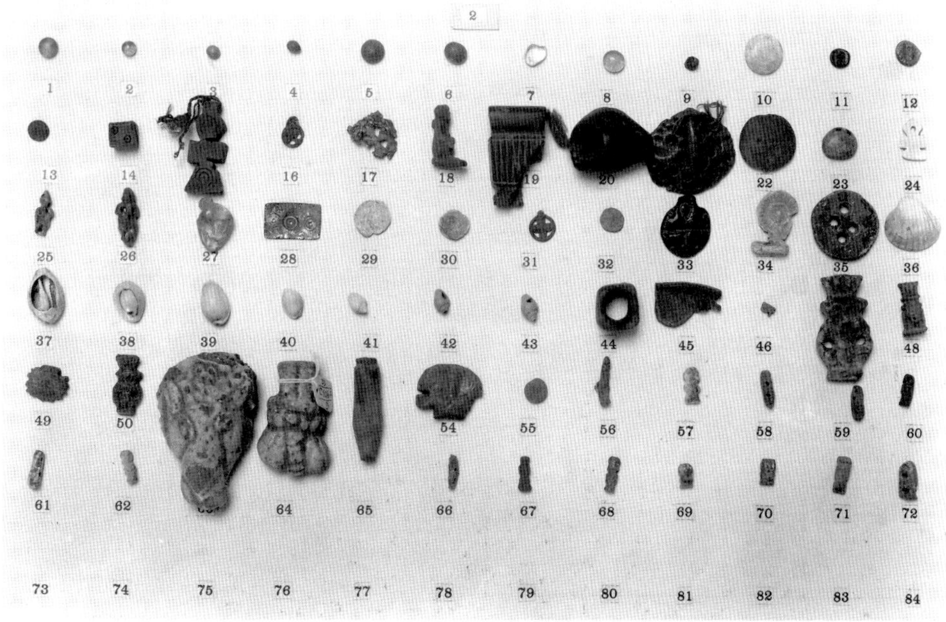

Fig. 13. Division album photograph (Kelsey Museum neg. no. 7.2526).

"Division Album I" (48 leaves bearing 269 annotated photographs)
"Division 1934/5 Album II" (53 leaves bearing 113 annotated photographs)

These two albums contain photographs taken for the divisions of finds from the Michigan excavations at Karanis, Soknopaiou Nesos, and Terenouthis. Photographs showing assemblages of objects, most often organized by types of material, are mounted in albums and annotated. The arrays of objects in the first album are mostly photographed against a background of black cloth (fig. 12); the second album also includes several grids of smaller objects (especially coins) photographed against a light background (fig. 13). The photographs are annotated, with individual objects numbered (sometimes with objects retained in Egypt further marked with an "x"), the numbers keyed to detailed photograph captions preserved elsewhere in the archive.

These albums are a crucial record of the Michigan expedition finds shortly after their excavation: they record objects in the condition in which they were found, or with some cleaning, but in many cases preserve objects since lost or deteriorated.

ties Service, subsequently dispersed to a number of museums in Cairo (most notably the Cairo Museum, the Coptic Museum, and the Agricultural Museum).

The "Peterson Manuscript"

> Enoch E. Peterson, "The Architecture and Topography of Karanis, 1928–1935," bound typescript with handwritten corrections and annotations in 3 volumes with supplementary binder of plates (vol. 1: xii + 393 pp.; vol. 2: pp. 394–867; index vol.: 361 pp.; plates volume: 113 5" × 7" b/w photographic prints + 4 leaves of index in binder). Manuscript completed in 1973; corrections, annotations, and supplementary material (indices and photographic illustrations) completed at some point(s) after the main manuscript was completed.

Another source for the Michigan Karanis excavations that has attained somewhat legendary status is a substantial unpublished manuscript completed by excavation director Enoch E. Peterson in 1973, essentially a report on the 1928–1935 seasons' work at Karanis, intended as a follow-up to the published volume on the 1924–1928 seasons.

Peterson's manuscript surveys the 1928–1935 excavations by "layer" (as identified by the excavators), and also by site area. Peterson supplied considerable detail about architecture and building technique, some detail about overall structures, areas, and their relationships, but rather less information about specific finds. So in this regard, the unpublished manuscript has sometimes come as a disappointment to researchers seeking information about individual objects.

It is not entirely accurate, in any case, to consider the Peterson manuscript as entirely "unpublished": it was used as the basis of the 1979 Kelsey Museum publication *Karanis Excavations of the University of Michigan in Egypt 1928–1935: Topography and Architecture* (Husselman 1979). This volume, subtitled "A Summary of the Reports of the Director, Enoch E. Peterson," was brought to publication by Elinor M. Husselman after Peterson's death in 1978, a heroic feat under the circumstances, carried out with the assistance of Louise Shier. Indeed Husselman and Shier can be seen as the relatively unsung heroes of the Michigan Karanis project; although neither of them worked at the site during the excavations, both put forth extraordinary efforts in bringing material from the excavation to publication, while facilitating the work of others on this material in the context of their respective positions with the University Library Papyrus Collection and the Kelsey Museum of Archaeology.

Peterson seems to have envisioned publication of his manuscript along the lines of the two earlier reports published in the University of Michigan Press

"Humanistic Series," with a full complement of plates and large-scale folding maps and plans. But the situation had changed dramatically between the original publications of the 1930s and the completion of Peterson's manuscript in 1973: the Michigan "Humanistic Series" had long since ceased publication, and resources were simply not available for a publication on the scale that Peterson's 800+-page manuscript would have required. Husselman was left with the unenviable task of reenvisioning Peterson's intentions into something that could be published with the resources available.

In her preface to the published volume, Husselman details the difficulties of the project and the compromises that were needed to bring it to publication. The greatest necessary sacrifices were in image quality.[4] Photographic illustrations were made from archival photographs but lost considerable detail in the process of halftone screening (although, given the process and paper, the photographic images are surprisingly legible, at least in the original printing of the book). Maps and plans were even more problematic. The large-scale folding plates of the earlier volumes were financially impractical for the 1979 publication. So larger maps and plans were broken up into smaller units: photographic negatives of the resulting sections of the originals were used to make 8" × 10" black-and-white prints for the individual publication plates. These prints were, in some cases, further elaborated on: larger-scale printed versions of street and structure numbers were added to some of the maps over the handwritten notations on the originals to provide more clarity for reference. As anyone who has used this volume will know, the maps and plans as printed are at a very small scale—the printing on maps and plans can be tiny and difficult to read, although nearly all legends and notations can be read with a magnifying glass, at least in the original printing of the book.

Husselman describes these issues frankly in her preface. She also writes rather self-deprecatingly of her own archaeological qualifications to prepare the volume, but here I think she does herself an injustice. Although not a field archaeologist either by training or by experience, Husselman knew the

[4] The issue of image quality is complicated by the varying processes used for different print runs of the book. The original 1979 printing by University Microfilms International for the University of Michigan Press used standard offset technique on book paper and has the most legible images. This seems to have been a relatively small print run, however, perhaps only 500 copies or fewer, and quickly sold out. The volume was later reprinted at least twice using xerographic or photocopy quality printing from microfilm onto copy paper, and the quality of images suffered greatly. Fine details on the maps in these later printings are largely illegible.

documentation of the Karanis excavations almost as well as Peterson himself. As a papyrologist, Husselman wrote articles in which she used the archaeological evidence from Karanis to situate groups of texts from the excavations.[5] She was, in effect, the true pioneer of the "text in context" approach to Karanis so important in recent work on the site. Perhaps more than anyone at the time, Husselman understood the Karanis excavation material well enough to edit Peterson's enormous and unwieldy manuscript into a manageable and publishable volume.

Husselman's publication substantially restructures Peterson's report: it briefly surveys the history of the site, the excavators' "layers," and the construction techniques used. But the bulk of the book covers the different types of structures at the site, pulling specific examples from Peterson's report and frequently placing them in the context of the surrounding buildings. As with Peterson's manuscript, the Husselman book does not give much information about specific finds of objects. The photographs and plans illustrating Husselman's book parallel those planned by Peterson, although the number of plates in the book is less than two-thirds of those proposed by Peterson, and the book's numbering of maps and plans does not correspond to the system used by Peterson.[6] Indeed, the plans that Peterson's manuscript references seem not to exist as such—they were intended to be compiled and redrawn from the larger site plans in the museum archives that the Husselman book uses in reduced form. The detailed set of indices in Peterson's manuscript is partly paralleled in the published book, but Husselman did not include anything corresponding to Peterson's extremely detailed "General Index" (pp. 1–108 of the index volume), which remains perhaps the most useful feature of the manuscript versus the published version. As an example from my own research, recourse to Peterson's General Index leads to a number of instances of traces of fires and burned contexts (under "Fire") at Karanis, information not easily found in Husselman's book.

The original manuscript of Peterson's report has always been available for consultation by researchers in the Kelsey Museum; this intention is stated in Husselman's publication and has been followed ever since. More recently, the manuscript has been scanned and will be made available in preliminary form, through the "Karanis Revealed" website upon the publication of the present volume.

[5] For more information about Elinor Husselman, and a bibliography, see the obituary notice in Wilfong 1996.

[6] The Peterson manuscript projected 280 plates and 119 maps and plans for publication, versus the 106 plates (containing 182 images) and 68 maps and plans published in Husselman's book.

Appendix. A Note on Field Numbers

Each find at Karanis was assigned a field number that indicates findspot and the season in which the find was made (Amundsen 1935).

Each field number is prefixed with the final two digits of the beginning year of the season (e.g., "24" for the 1924–1925 season, "25" for the 1925–1926 season, etc.). The next element consists of an alphanumeric encoding of occupational level designation (if any), structure or area number, and room or sub-area. As discussed elsewhere in this volume (pp. 36–43 and 82–83), the excavators identified levels as "A" (most recent) to "F" (earliest), although the "A" was usually not included in field numbers. "S" denotes "Street" (so "BS" indicates a street in the B level). Rooms were identified with capital letters. An asterisk appended to a structure, area, or room indicates a find made underneath a room or between levels. Superscript numbers indicate subdivisions of rooms or bin numbers.

Individual finds are indicated by letters. Finds (excepting pottery vessels) are designated with capital A–Z (excluding I), followed by AI–ZI, AII–ZII, etc. (AA–AZ, AAA–AAZ, etc. in the first two seasons. Pottery vessels are then designated with lowercase a–z, further finds following a similar ai–zi or aa–az system.

Thus, 24-114D-a is the field number for the first find of pottery in structure 114, room D, in level A, from the 1924–1925 season. And 29-B188A^{8}-A is the field number for the first find in the eighth subdivision of room A of structure B188 in level B from the 1929–1930 season.

Field numbers for surface finds are sometimes given as "X," so 27-X is a surface find made in the 1927–1928 season, although years of surface finds are often not indicated. "SG" is used for finds (assumed to be surface finds) made in the absence of the excavators by the summer site guards, so 27-SG-Z is the 25th find by the summer guards registered in 1927.

Field numbers for Dimé finds follow a system similar to those for Karanis, except for the use of Roman numerals to identify one of the two areas excavated: 31-II 202F-y identifies the 24th find of pottery in room F, structure 202 in area II from the 1931–1932 season.

Field numbers for Terenouthis finds from the brief 1935 season use a completely different system: number indicating area on the site followed by a letter indicating sub-area (if any), followed by letter indicating type of find and number indicating individual find. Thus, 10-A95 is the 95th stela from area 10, 3B-A7 is the seventh shabti figure from tomb B in area 3.

Bibliography

Amundsen, L. 1935. *Greek Ostraca in the University of Michigan Collection: Part I, Texts*. University of Michigan Studies, Humanistic Series, 34. Ann Arbor: University of Michigan Press.

Husselman, E. M. 1952. "The Granaries of Karanis." *Transactions of the American Philological Association* 83:56–73.

Husselman, E. M. 1953. "The Dovecotes of Karanis." *Transactions of the American Philological Association* 84:81–91.

Husselman, E. M. 1979. *Karanis Excavations of the University of Michigan in Egypt 1928–1935: Topography and Architecture. A Summary of the Reports of the Director, Enoch E. Peterson.* Kelsey Museum of Archaeology Studies, 5. Ann Arbor: University of Michigan Press.

Wilfong, T. G. 1996. "Elinor Mullett Husselman." *Bulletin of the American Society of Papyrologists* 33:5–10.

Silent Movies from the Michigan Expedition to Egypt

T. G. Wilfong

Among the archival documentation generated by the Michigan Karanis project, the silent film footage of the expedition has achieved near legendary status in the Kelsey Museum community and beyond.[1] Hours of footage have long been known to exist, and rumors of their contents have abounded, but until recently most knowledge of this material has been limited to a roughly ten-minute video compilation of clips pulled together for the landmark 1983 "Karanis" exhibition at the Kelsey Museum. Stories of this film footage and its vicissitudes over time have long persisted, but a serious examination of the surviving material and its context reveals a fascinating glimpse of what might have been: a projected documentary, or even a feature film, about the Michigan Karanis excavations, the joint brainchild of Francis W. Kelsey and photographer George R. Swain.

The fact that there are films of the Karanis excavation at all is a testimony to Francis W. Kelsey's vision and his openness to new technologies in the documentation and promotion of archaeology. Kelsey wanted the expedition to be as up-to-date as possible in terms of documentation, so provided for a full photographic record of the excavation, as was becoming the norm for fieldwork in Egypt at the time. Less typical (and more indicative of his innovative ideas about archaeology) was Kelsey's insistence on the use of aerial photographs of the site: the Michigan team hired flyers from the British Royal Air Force to do a photographic flyover of Karanis and a few other Fayum sites (including ancient Philadelphia). The extraordinarily detailed images that resulted not only helped Michigan settle on Karanis as their site of choice but also proved an ongoing resource for planning the excavation and understanding the site as a whole.

[1] This article is excerpted from a longer essay, based on a lecture I gave at the Kelsey Museum of Archaeology on 26 June 2012 as part of the programming for the exhibition "A Man of Many Parts: The Life and Legacy of Francis Willey Kelsey." The original essay placed the Karanis films into a wider context of silent film culture and Kelsey's own relationship with the movies. Thanks to Elaine K. Gazda and Sebastián Encina for useful background information; this article would not have been possible without John G. Pedley's biography of Francis W. Kelsey.

To the end of being up-to-date in Michigan's documentation of the site and the archaeological activities there, Kelsey also wanted motion picture footage. In 1924, Kelsey had discussed this possibility with photographer George R. Swain before the excavation had begun (Pedley 2012, 398). The attitude of both men seemed to be not to rush into anything but to study the situation, and Swain expended some effort to educate himself about motion picture techniques and equipment. But nothing else was done about it in Michigan's first seasons at Karanis. Indeed, the Karanis project proved in many ways overwhelming to Kelsey and the Michigan team. Much more was discovered than expected, and dealing with both the results of the excavations and the logistics of maintaining a project in Egypt turned out to be far more complicated than anticipated. Michigan was also involved in a number of other fieldwork projects under Kelsey's aegis, and his attention was divided. Kelsey did maintain a keen interest in the Karanis project in particular—one can glimpse his pleasure in the well-known photograph of his visit to Karanis on Christmas day 1926. In that same year, the Michigan project at Carthage was documented in movies taken by a Pathé Exchange crew: some 24 reels of film were donated to the University by Pathé (Pedley 2012, 361 n. 251), and this may have reminded Kelsey and Swain of their plans for films of the work at Karanis. But there were more pressing matters, and nothing was done about filming at the site.

No further discussion of the issue of motion pictures of Karanis seems to have taken place until 6 May 1927. Kelsey was by this time in the hospital with his final illness. But in his diary he records asking Swain: "'Shall we develop movie photography in our work in Egypt?' Swain replied, 'Yes, much informed on the subject since we first considered it in 1924. If we do go into movie photography we agree that it must be on a strictly professional basis, with the best equipment. "Baby" camera not adequate'" (Pedley 2012, 398). This appears to have been one of Kelsey's last professional conversations, and he died a week later on 14 May 1927. Perhaps this final conversation with Swain took on the force of a deathbed request to the photographer. In any case, motion picture filming at Karanis began the following year, under Swain's direction. The Michigan team did invest in a professional-type camera, not a toy, but, unfortunately, not in a professional location crew or experienced cameraman.

Between 1928 and 1930, with some possible additional filming in 1935, Swain filmed about four hours of motion picture footage at Karanis, along with about fifteen minutes filmed at Kom Abou Billou (ancient Terenouthis) before the brief Michigan excavation at the site in April 1935. From the looks of it, film was quite

Fig. 14. Field intertitle (reel IIa).

Fig. 15. Scene of work on site (reel IIb).

possibly developed on site, although it may also have had to wait until the return to Michigan. From the start, there was the intention to use the raw footage from Karanis as the basis for a documentary. Some scene titles or intertitles in the film footage were clearly made in the field, typed using the field typewriter with its distinctive face on cloudy paper, or perhaps cardboard from reused binders (fig. 14).

The purpose of film footage was clearly documentary, but not in the way a modern audience might think of as a "documentary" film. There are no shots of finds as they happen, nor are there any good *in situ* sequences of objects being taken out of the ground. What we see instead is general activity on the site (mostly involving the Egyptian workers), shots of individual buildings, and broad panoramas (fig. 15). Swain himself was a pioneer of the use of panoramic still photography for the documentation of archaeological sites,[2] which may help account for the sheer volume of motion picture pans in the Karanis footage. We also get a lot of what we might call local color: the environment and inhabitants around Karanis and the overall landscape (fig. 16).

Swain was an outstanding still photographer—he understood his cameras and media very well. His Karanis still photographs are wonderful examples of the use of photography for the documentation of archaeological sites and processes. Motion picture photography was a very different art, however, and we can see Swain learning on the job, in effect. Exposure was, in particular, a major problem,

[2] Swain's panoramas were the subject of a 2000 exhibition at the Kelsey Museum, curated by Robin Meador-Woodruff, "Surrounded by the View: Panoramic Photographs from the Kelsey Museum Archives"; see the brief notice "Exhibition of Panoramics" in the *Kelsey Museum Newsletter*, Fall 1999, 2.

Fig. 16. Water buffalos near Karanis (reel Ia).

Fig. 17. Intertitle (reel Ia).

and the addition of motion—both the motion of the subjects and the motion of the camera itself—was a challenge, especially given the very changeable conditions in the field. The frequent dust storms at Karanis (documented in one extraordinary sequence of film), which made still photography difficult enough, were particularly inhospitable for motion picture filming. The results of the Michigan expedition foray into movies are very mixed indeed.

Once the film made it back to Ann Arbor, it is clear that there was some attempt to organize it and select portions for some kind of documentary, even a feature-length film. A new level of "professional" intertitles was introduced at some point—the more traditional white type on a black background that was standard in silent film of the time (fig. 17). There is also some evidence of editing in the footage as it survives today that may date to this early period. Precisely what was envisioned for the resulting film is unclear. It may have been intended only for internal use, although the level of titling suggests a more popular, public focus.

The Karanis footage was made at a time when film as a whole was beginning to undergo a major transformation: silent films were beginning to make way for sound films, talking pictures. Experiments in sound film had been going on for nearly as long as film itself, but technology to add synchronous sound directly to the projected film was finally perfected and became the standard. *The Jazz Singer* (1927) was the first widely shown feature-length film with synch sound dialogue, and its popularity made it, and sound film, a sensation. Suddenly the world of film was in turmoil: planned silent films were scrapped, stage plays were quickly adapted for film, and features in production were hastily having sound sequences added. Silent film was, for mass audiences anyway, quickly on its way out. So the Michigan

Karanis team would have had to factor in sound if their ambitions extended to public presentation in a theater, and probably in any case sound would have been a necessity for a university audience.

At some point in the 1930s, work on the Karanis film seems to have ceased. It may be that the prospect of adding sound to a silent film project was too daunting. More likely it was a combination of the overwhelming amount of material—artifactual and archival—coming back to Ann Arbor from Karanis and the decreasing financial resources available to deal with this material. Michigan no longer had Kelsey as its dynamic fundraiser to bring in money for archaeological projects, but the Great Depression decreased available funds in any case. Although the film from Karanis was occasionally screened on an ad hoc basis, it was not until much later that anything further was done with it.

As was the practice of the time, the Karanis film positives were made on cellulose nitrate stock, an industry standard in the silent film era. Its advantages were many: the material was relatively cheap and provided film with good detail and strong contrasts. But the benefits of using cellulose nitrate stock were offset by very serious disadvantages. Cellulose nitrate film deteriorates and decomposes very easily, turning into an acidic-smelling mush. Even worse, this film is also highly flammable, sometimes explosive, and can burn even under water. Cellulose nitrate film is extremely dangerous as it ages and must be stored at low temperatures for preservation and safety needs. In spite of these dangers, the Karanis film somehow survived in a viewable form, neither deteriorating nor exploding. The original cellulose nitrate stock was stored in the Kelsey Museum but ultimately moved offsite.[3] Before the original film was moved, an acetate "safety" film master was made from the original. This is a common practice for films on volatile cellulose nitrate stock; the resulting film is safe and stable, but there can be some loss of detail in the transfer (although it is not always clear if such detail loss is due to the difference in stock or deterioration already present in the original). For all practical purposes, the acetate safety film transfer of the Karanis films is now our primary source for this footage.

From the acetate safety film, the Karanis footage was transferred to video tape at some point in the early 1980s, done in preparation for the major 1983 Kelsey Museum exhibition on Karanis, curated by Elaine K. Gazda and described

[3] It is unclear whether the original cellulose nitrate film still survives, but even if so, it is unlikely that it exists in a viewable condition. The disposition and whereabouts of the original film negatives are unrecorded.

elsewhere in this volume. As a result of the transfer to video, a listing of the contents of the footage was compiled, mostly using information from the existing intertitles and timings from the video. Brief excerpts from the video transfer were compiled together into a short (approximately ten-minute) video with added musical soundtrack (intended to evoke ancient flute music), shown on continuous loop in the exhibition galleries and later used in classroom and public presentations on Karanis. It is this video compilation that has been the only available source for the Karanis silent film footage until recently; the full video transfers and master acetate films have been in storage and not available.

In preparation for "Karanis Revealed," Sebastián Encina patiently supervised the digitization of about half of the videos, roughly two hours of footage. I have subdivided this material into clips, based on the division suggested both by subject matter and the two levels of intertitles. Short excerpts of four of the clips appeared on the interactive iPad presentations in the gallery for both phases of "Karanis Revealed," the clips used for the second part of the exhibition accompanied by a randomized soundtrack of ambient sounds from Karanis in 2010, recorded and mixed by artist John Kannenberg.[4] I further presented a compilation of about 25 minutes' worth of clips in the public lecture for the Kelsey on which the present essay is based. Subsequently, thanks to the efforts of Sebastián Encina, the Karanis footage has been digitized anew, this time from the acetate safety film, providing clips of considerably higher quality than the older video transfer. Ultimately, the Kelsey Museum will make this material available online.

A review of the digitized footage from Karanis allows us to at least imagine what was intended for the final film to be made from this footage. The two levels of intertitling make clear the basic intentions for the film and give clues as to the intended ordering of individual sequences. Knowledge of the conventions and tropes of silent film provides further help: the Karanis film would follow standard narrative paths rather than blaze new artistic trails.

A number of clips were clearly envisioned as beginnings to a longer film: general pans and surveys of the site of Karanis, sequences titled variously "Karanis" and "The Deserted City." These provide an overview of the site and help orient the viewer (presumably with the help of still shots of maps and plans). A substantial amount of the footage was devoted to showing archaeological activity on the site,

[4] See John Kannenberg's article later in this volume about the major project resulting from his Karanis field recordings.

and one can see the raw material for a basic overview of archaeological process: workers dig, take dirt to be sieved, and then put the sieved dirt into railway carts for disposal away from the site. The film also gives a sense of the sheer numbers of Egyptian workers hired by the Michigan team, and the titles given to these sequences present the work as a team effort (e.g., "We Uncover Buried Karanis"). The Americans and Europeans on the project appear much less frequently; we apparently see Enoch Peterson in a sequence called "On the Hill and at Camp" going to and from the site. The Michigan team's beloved "dig dog" Plupy makes cameos in a number of sequences.[5]

Surveys of the site and footage of workers on the site are mixed in with more specific footage of individual structures at Karanis: so the houses and temples are documented in pans as well as with shots of workers in and around them. But viewers hoping for shots of actual discoveries or even scenes set inside ancient buildings will be disappointed. It is clear that the motion picture camera setup was fairly immobile: Swain's eternal pans aside, there was no practical way to get the camera into the tight, small doorways and corridors of the remains of Karanis, and certainly no practical way to light such scenes. But there are scenes of workers going in and out of structures, and many of workers clearly posing in doorways for the camera or clambering over mud-brick buildings. These sequences are extraordinarily useful for getting a sense of space at Karanis: how the architecture looks and functions with people in and around it brings the site to life, in effect—not just in terms of scale but in terms of how people functioned in its environment. The houses that were the focus of individual sequences were mostly buildings from the "C" level: houses C63, C68, various dovecotes in C-level houses, and the elaborate granary complex C123. Both the North Temple and the Temple of Pnepheros and Petesuchos were featured in sequences, one of which (with a later, white-on-black title) was clearly intended for a final film. The topography of the site is seen in a more general sequence, with a later title "General Scenes from Old Karanis": mostly a compilation of scenes of Egyptian workers, this sequence also includes a pan of the side of the mound, giving a sense of the height and layering of the ancient Kom.

A number of sequences reflecting the wider environment of Karanis and the lives of the inhabitants around the site were clearly envisioned as being part of the final film from the beginning (as attested by their field titling). Some document

[5] For Plupy and the other Karanis dig pets, see Wilfong 2013.

something of the system of canals around Karanis: "Our Water Supply," "The Wadi Abdalla Canal," and "We Build Dams." (The Michigan team helped the local inhabitants shore up canal banks and dams after a major canal break in 1925.)[6] "Wheels that Sing" documents water wheels in use, while "Water Buffalos at Home" shows some of the animal inhabitants of the area. "High Winds from Sahara Way" is the surprisingly dramatic documentation of a sand storm, one of the many that plagued the Michigan project throughout its duration.

How to structure and end the film was already being envisioned in the field. Sequences of Karanis and environs at dusk, "At Close of a Winter's Day" and "When Evening Comes" among them, suggest that the completed film might have followed the Karanis project over the course of a hypothetical day, ending with scenes of sunsets over the site. (This would have more or less been the latest filming could have gone, in that the team clearly did not have the lighting or expertise necessary for nighttime sequences or interior scenes in the dig house.) Such an ending would have been consistent with silent dramas of the time. But another, humorous ending also seems to have been a possibility. In a sequence titled in the field as "Good-Bye," we see Egyptian workers piling onto the expedition's beleaguered truck in front of the dig house. This may have been a joke in part reflecting the times: 1920s college stunts involving the packing of as many people as possible into cars, phone booths, etc. would have been familiar to the Michigan team. Once the truck was packed with as many people as possible (and far more than was safe), it drove off, followed by the camera down the long, winding road away from Karanis, until it was no longer visible. Such an ending would have paralleled more the silent comedies of the time. Drama or comedy: it is hard to know which way the planned documentary would have gone.

This, then, seems to have been the general plan for the Karanis documentary as decipherable from the digitized footage. A number of sequences consist of film of still images made from archival material—building plans and object photographs mostly. This suggests the intention to add these shots to the moving footage of individual structures seen in the digitized materials to provide fuller records of the buildings in question: the finished sequences devoted to individual structures would have shown not just the pans of standing architecture and the shots of workers moving in and around them but also plans and sketches, along with images

[6] Documented in archival photographs, negatives 655–660.

of objects found in the structures, to give as comprehensive a picture as possible. Further general site views could have provided backdrops for voiceovers or superimposed titles and would have increased the choices for the compilers (perhaps a reason for the frequent duplication of very similar shots in the footage as well). If we assume a planned documentary of 60 to 90 minutes, the roughly 240 minutes of footage plus further titles, maps, plans, and still images would have provided ample material for the finished film.

Or, rather, it would have provided enough material for a feature film if the quality had been better. Although it is difficult to assess from the digitized video alone, it is evident that the majority of the footage is either overexposed or underexposed (sometimes both extremes occurring in the same sequence). Although the Karanis still photographs, largely the work of Swain,[7] are in general beautiful examples of archaeological field photography made under often-difficult conditions, the motion picture sequences are a different matter. Not only is exposure a constant problem in this footage, but focus frequently becomes an issue as well. Even allowing for deterioration of the original cellulose nitrate stock and the successive loss of detail and quality in the transfers to acetate and video, it is unlikely that the bulk of the Karanis footage would have been of adequate quality for any sort of feature or documentary. In some ways, the footage is better suited for viewing at a smaller scale—video on a television as in the 1983 exhibition or small-scale digitized video on the iPads of the 2011 exhibition. The original film project may have been abandoned simply because the quality of the resulting footage was disappointing.

It is difficult to judge how much time and effort should be invested in further restoring the Karanis silent films or whether the resources necessary for doing so would be better spent in digitizing more critical archival material from the Karanis excavations. At a minimum, the digitized footage from the acetate safety masters will be made freely available in raw form online. Given Kelsey's own openness to new technologies for the documentation and promotion of archaeological excavation, as witnessed by the very existence of this film footage, I think he would have approved of a free digital release along the lines we have planned. Ultimately, wide availability of the original Karanis footage may someday allow production of a documentary approximating Francis Kelsey's original vision.

[7] A small but significant number (62) were by J. Anthony Chubb, well known for his work at other sites in Egypt, while many Karanis archival photographs remain uncredited, although these are usually presumed to be Swain's work.

Bibliography

Pedley, J. G. 2012. *The Life and Work of Francis Willey Kelsey: Archaeology, Antiquity and the Arts*. Ann Arbor: University of Michigan Press.

Wilfong, T. G. 2013. "Dig Dogs and Camp Cats at Karanis: The Animals of the 1924–1935 University of Michigan Expedition to Egypt." In B. J. Collins and P. Michalowski, eds., *Beyond Hatti: A Tribute to Gary Beckman*. Atlanta: Lockwood Press, 325–341.

The Michigan Papyrology Collection and Karanis

Adam P. Hyatt

The University of Michigan Papyrus Collection is the largest collection of ancient documents on papyrus in the Western Hemisphere and among the largest in the world. Among the more than 7,000 inventory numbers and ca. 17,000 individual fragments (many inventory numbers include multiple fragments), it includes many documents from Karanis as well as other parts of Egypt. The papyri range in date from ca. 1200 BC to AD 1000, with the majority dating to the Graeco-Roman period (300 BC–AD 600). Most of the texts are Greek, but languages from all of the different peoples who lived in Egypt during this time are represented, including Hieratic, Demotic, Latin, Aramaic, and Arabic. Also included in this collection are writing materials other than papyri, such as wax and wooden tablets, ostraka, lead, and parchment. The collection includes works of classical literature, religious and magical texts, scientific writings, public records, and private texts such as personal letters.

The Papyrology Collection resulted from the energy and direction of Francis Kelsey, a Latin professor at the University of Michigan in the early 20th century. He saw the importance of having a teaching collection of archaeological objects, including papyri, as these provide a direct and unprecedented view into the ancient world and the lives of its inhabitants. In fact, it was Kelsey's desire to establish a teaching collection for the university that eventually led him to begin excavations at Karanis.

Prior to the excavations, Kelsey began amassing papyri for the university through private purchases. With few exceptions, papyrology collections around the globe have been assembled primarily through purchases of documents from dealers. From 1920 to the mid-1930s, Kelsey's purchases of papyri occurred mainly through a consortium of academic institutions, led by the British Museum.[1] Once papyri made their way into the hands of dealers in Egypt, they were sent to the British Museum, where they underwent some amount of conservation and were examined for content. From there, the papyri were distributed to the member

[1] Other members included Cornell, Princeton, Columbia, Wisconsin, and the Geneva and Oslo collections.

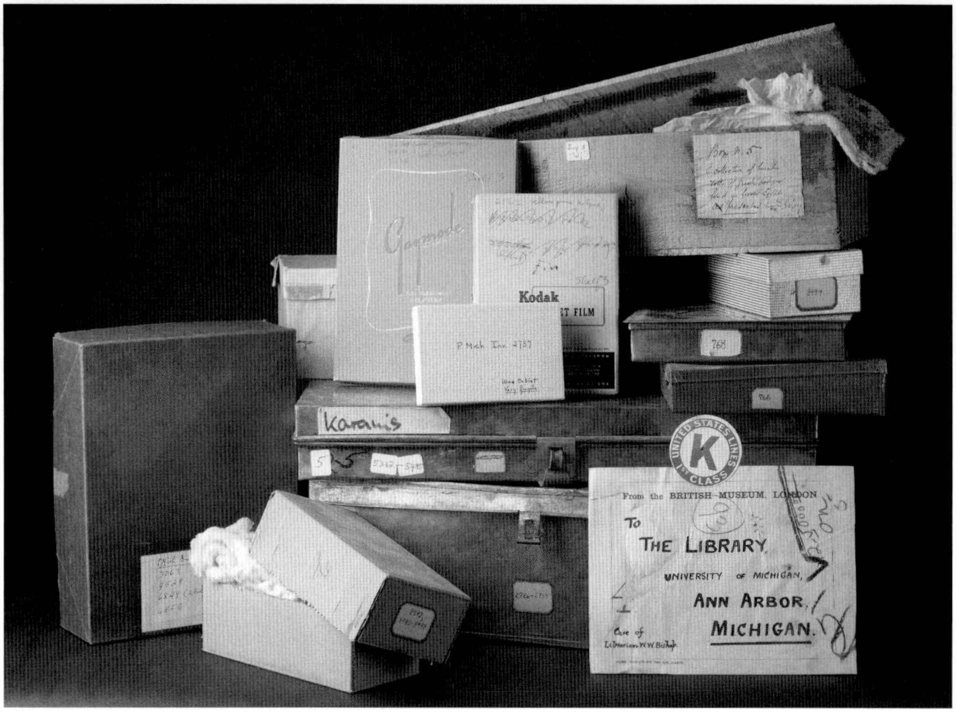

Fig. 18. Boxes used to transport papyri from Egypt to Ann Arbor in the 1920s and early 1930s. Photograph by Randal Stegmeyer, 2010 (courtesy of the University of Michigan Library Papyrology Collection).

institutions based upon how much money each institution contributed and what types of texts each institution requested (fig. 18).

Although this process may have served the purposes of the many university collections at the time, it completely obliterated any contextual information that may have been derived from the papyri. In most cases, these dealers acquired the papyri from Egyptian farmers. Papyri were unearthed, but little or no information was recorded as to where they came from, and their archaeological context was forever lost. Moreover, once papyri were in the hands of dealers or even the British Museum, groups of associated texts that were discovered together were most often divided and distributed to various institutions. In many cases, even fragments belonging to the same individual papyrus were divided between institutions.

In the process of purchasing papyri, Kelsey had also witnessed firsthand how the practices of collecting had destroyed Graeco-Roman sites. Therefore, in 1924 he decided to undertake careful excavations at Karanis in order to fulfill his vision of "the reconstruction of the environment of life in the Graeco-Roman period . . . and the increase of exact knowledge rather than the amassing of collections" (Gazda 2004, 4). This vision, as it was employed at Karanis, "represented a revolutionary, paradigmatic change in the approach to the Graeco-Roman past in Egypt" (Gagos 2005, 171). Now as papyri were recovered, their archaeological contexts were being recorded for the first time. The ancient town of Karanis was excavated systematically, and papyri and other artifacts were recorded according to the house, room, and level in which they were unearthed. These data made possible the creation of detailed maps and plans, which still allow researchers to pinpoint where objects were found and their relation to architecture and other objects.

The Karanis excavations took place between 1924 and 1935 and yielded over 4,000 papyri and 6,000 ostraca, included in a total of over 68,000 archaeological objects. Initially, all objects from the excavation that came to Michigan were housed in what would ultimately be known as the Kelsey Museum of Archaeology; the papyri were eventually transferred to the University Library to form the core of its Papyrology Collection. Although many of the papyri were returned to Cairo in 1954 as part of the original terms of the excavation, the U-M Papyrology Collection still houses approximately 2,500 fragments of these papyri. In addition, pictures and negatives of many of the pieces that were returned also remain.

This collection of excavated papyri, in conjunction with the other archaeological material from Karanis, truly sets the U-M Papyrology Collection apart in that researchers have the unique opportunity to reconstruct and populate an ancient community in terms of individuals, families, administrative organization, and larger social networks. One document in particular that best exemplifies the potential for this type of study is the Karanis Tax Register (P.Mich.inv. 4172—object **49** in the "Karanis Revealed" exhibition described below). Dating to AD 173–174, this document records the collecting of taxes paid by individuals, and actually lists many of the residents of the ancient town and how much they paid either as a poll tax or in land taxes. This document is invaluable in its own right for understanding such issues as taxation, demographics, and land use, to name a few. But when considered in conjunction with the architectural remains and other documents and objects from Karanis, the document provides an unprecedented view into the organization of this town and its inhabitants.

Papyrologists have been working on this collection ever since the first pieces arrived in 1920 (fig. 19), yet much work remains to be done. Currently approximately 10,000 fragments from the U-M Papyrology Collection still remain unpublished. Moreover, only about a third of the collection has received

Fig. 19. Example of how unconserved papyrus fragments were shipped and stored (P.Mich.inv. 6827). Photograph by Randal Stegmeyer, 2010 (courtesy of the University of Michigan Library Papyrology Collection).

any conservation. In order to preserve this collection and to encourage and facilitate its study by students and researchers around the globe, the U-M Papyrology Collection has been digitized and made available online to the public through the Advanced Papyrological Information System (APIS).[2] Here anyone can search our papyri and access high-resolution images, descriptions, and translations, a great research tool for learning more about Karanis and Graeco-Roman Egypt.

Bibliography

Gagos, T., Gates, J. E., and Wilburn, A. T. 2005. "Material Culture and Texts of Graeco-Roman Egypt: Creating Context, Debating Meaning." *Bulletin of the American Society of Papyrologists* 42:171–188.

Gazda, E. K. 2004. *Karanis: An Egyptian Town in Roman Times. Discoveries of the University of Michigan Expedition to Egypt (1924–1935)*, 2nd ed. with new introduction and bibliography by T. G. Wilfong. Ann Arbor: Kelsey Museum of Archaeology.

[2] http://www.lib.umich.edu/papyrus-collection/advanced-papyrological-information-system-apis

Karanis Findspots and Stratigraphy

Thomas Landvatter

The stratigraphy of Karanis has always been problematic. The Michigan excavators divided the site into six "occupation" levels labeled "A" through "F." Levels "E" and "D" were dated from the late 1st century BC to the early 1st century AD, from the late Ptolemaic to the early Roman period; level "C" to the mid-1st to early 2nd centuries AD; level "B" from the mid-2nd to late 3rd centuries AD; and level "A" from the late 3rd to the mid-5th centuries AD (Husselman 1979). However, there are two major problems with this schema: (1) these levels were based on architectural change rather than true soil stratigraphy; and (2) they were applied site-wide in a well-meaning attempt to examine change across the whole of the settlement. Cultural practices, environmental factors, and the nature of archaeological deposition prevent this from being an effective manner of examining the settlement. Houses were built and rebuilt at different rates as the sand blew in from the desert, filling up houses with debris mixed in with the rubbish residents were depositing themselves; thus, the "levels" proposed by the excavators cannot be universally applied site-wide; the levels are only consistent within a contiguous architectural area.

Although the excavators did note the findspots of objects with far greater precision than most excavations of the time, the overall quality of recordkeeping betrays the age of the excavation. Objects were associated with a room of the structure in which they were found (Husselman 1979). Each house was given a number, preceded by a letter indicating the "level" to which it belonged; rooms were identified with another letter following the house number. As an example, B224C indicates level B, house 224, room C. Individual objects were assigned an upper case letter (e.g., A, B, C, etc.), while whole vessels were given a lower case one (e.g., a, b, c, etc.); sherds were not recorded unless they were ostraka. For instance, the well-known "rag doll" on display (KM 26415) was designated B224C-A; that is, level B, house 224, object A. The ceramics have proved particularly problematic to work with, as only few examples were taken back to Ann Arbor, and all were catalogued using a ceramic typology the key to which has only very recently been rediscovered. For example, B224B-a (level B, house 224, room B, pottery find "a") was simply listed as "517, XXIII, c, i."

Fig. 20. C-level structures, rooms containing objects filled in with crosshatch.

The published pottery corpus (Johnson 1981), which presents only a portion of the excavated pottery, makes no references to the earlier typology.

On occasion, the excavators note a more specific area within a room in which an object was found. Normally, no distinctions are made between artifacts found in the fill and those found on the floor; on occasion there is a note marking an object as "high in the fill." Often rooms are also given two separate designations: one regular entry and one with a "*" next to the room number. Thus there is both a context "B224B" and a "B224B*." This "*" is meant to designate a more specific area of the room and is often explained in a footnote (e.g., "under the stairs," "in a niche on the north wall"), but many times there is no specific explanation. B224B*, for instance, has no such explanation.

It is instructive to examine a single housing block to see how this system was put into practice. The block in question lies at the extreme southeast of the excavated area, in sector H11–H12 and at the edge of the area destroyed by the *sebakhin*. Occupation of the insula is evident in the C, B, and A levels (Husselman 1979, 7–10). In the C level, the block was comprised of "houses" C184, C187, C188, C189, C191; in the B layer, of B224, B226, B227, B228, B229, B231, and B232; and in the A layer, of A414, A416, A417, A418, A419, A421, and A422. Levels B and A used a combination of new construction and reuse of structures from previous levels. Large portions in both C and B levels have no objects ascribed to them; in the A level, there are no attributed finds, though portions of the earlier levels remained in use. In level C, finds are only recorded in houses C184 (rooms A, B, and D), C188 (rooms B and C), C189 (rooms, A, D, E, and G). The rooms that contained objects are filled in with crosshatch in figure 20. As can be seen, this leaves a significant portion of the insula seemingly barren in the C level.

The situation in the B level is slightly more complex. Here there were two separate designations, B and B*. Most recorded rooms had both B and B* designations (B224A, B, and C; B227A; B228A and B), while two had only recorded finds for the B* level (B229L*; B232K*), and only one had material attributed exclusively to the B level (B231K). In figure 21, those rooms with objects in the B layer are marked with parallel lines. Again, however, significant portions of the insula are recorded as having no objects.

There is no overlap between these two levels: buildings that contained objects in the C level have none in the B level, and vice versa. In addition, those rooms that have material dated to the B level are structures that underwent significant architectural modification from the C level; rooms that largely kept the C-level structure intact had objects assigned to them only in that level. Together, the B- and C-level artifact attributions cover the majority of the insula. The reason for this pattern can be found in the preliminary report of the seasons from 1924 to 1928, in reference to house 242:

> A new number was not given to the house of the B period. Wherever in the last period the earlier forms of the rooms were unchanged, as in rooms A, B, G, and H, the same letter applies to both A and B periods of occupation. The objects found in the lower levels, however, have been noted as coming from the earlier occupation. (Boak and Peterson 1931, 44 n. 1)

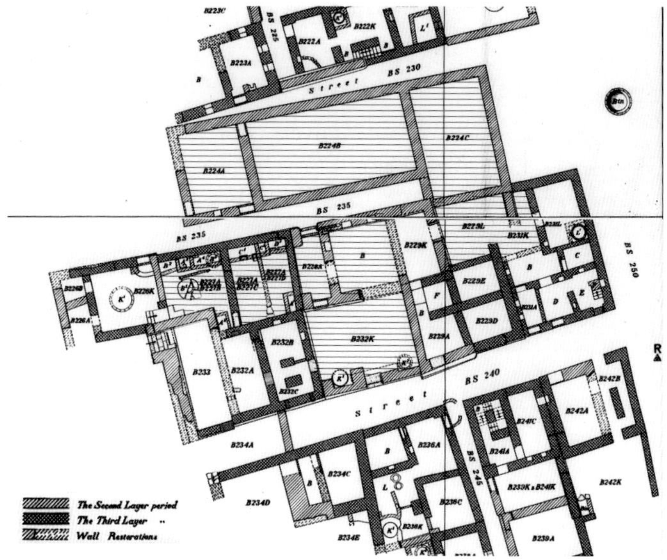

Fig. 21. B-level structures, rooms containing objects filled with parallel lines.

Though never explained in the full unpublished report (described above, pp. 20–22), this system seems to hold true for the later excavation seasons. The house numbers change throughout the insula, but letters assigned to rooms are maintained across architectural levels if there is no significant architectural change, while rooms that are restructured are assigned a new letter. In this insula at least, then, objects are not assigned to a proper stratigraphic level but are only associated with the most recent "level" of architectural change. This association, however, can be viewed as significant since any architectural change would also likely require a restructuring of the existing floor. Thus it makes sense, for instance, that no artifacts are attributed to C187, as that structure was completely dismantled and rebuilt as B228A-B and B232K. However, since there is no real stratigraphy, it is impossible to associate material labeled as from the C level solely with that level or labeled as B solely with B. Material throughout the insula has a possible association with the A, B, or C levels, as well as post-abandonment intrusions, regardless of the "level" assigned by the excavators. A high percentage of the artifacts from Karanis were likely deposited during the process of abandonment and in the post-abandonment period, rather than during the actual habitation of the site, and so may be significantly later in date than has previously presumed.

Bibliography

Boak, A. E. B., and Peterson, E. E. 1931. *Karanis: Topographical and Architectural Report of Excavations during the Seasons 1924–28*. University of Michigan Studies, Humanistic Series, 25. Ann Arbor: University of Michigan Press.

Husselman, E. M. 1979. *Karanis Excavations of the University of Michigan in Egypt 1928–1935: Topography and Architecture. A Summary of the Reports of the Director, Enoch E. Peterson*. Kelsey Museum of Archaeology Studies, 5. Ann Arbor: University of Michigan Press.

Johnson, B. 1981. *Pottery from Karanis: Excavations of the University of Michigan*. Kelsey Museum of Archaeology Studies, 7. Ann Arbor: University of Michigan Press.

ARTIFACTS

Artifacts found by the University of Michigan team at Karanis and related sites are, in some ways, our most immediate form of contact with the 1924–1935 excavations. The objects in Ann Arbor, ceded to the University of Michigan in a formal division of finds with the Egyptian Antiquities Service, are divided between the Kelsey Museum of Archaeology and the University Library Papyrology Collection and form key components of both collections. The 140 objects described in the following pages illustrate many aspects of Karanis and the Michigan excavations at the site but represent only a tiny fraction of the overall finds from the project.

Karanis Revealed: Artifacts from the Exhibition

T. G. Wilfong and Andrew W. S. Ferrara

The exhibition "Karanis Revealed" appeared in two parts, the first with an emphasis on earlier material from the site and the problems faced by the excavators, and the second with a focus on the latest material from the excavations and new directions in research. The checklist of artifacts from the exhibition that follows integrates both parts into a whole, with expansions of texts written for the exhibition and supplementary images and graphics from the exhibition.

A Priest from Karanis

The Kelsey Museum's well-known "Seated Dignitary" statue is, in fact, an Egyptian-styled representation of a priest from the early Roman period (later 1st century AD), excavated in 1928 at Karanis (fig. 22).

Fig. 22. Statue of a priest, **1**, not long after discovery (Kelsey Museum neg. no. 5.3717).

The statue, carved from black basalt, dates between AD 50 and 100. The figure is classically Egyptian in its formality and frontal, symmetrical orientation, but its proportions are not those of classical ancient Egyptian art—for example, the head is bigger than one would expect. Art historians have sometimes criticized the sculpture on these grounds, but in fact the Kelsey Museum statue is an important example of Egyptian traditional sculpture in its very late stages, all the more valuable because of its archaeological context.

The figure wears a traditional Egyptian short kilt but also a sash across the chest; its shaved head and costume show the man to have been a priest. The statue was found in a courtyard near the South Temple at Karanis, and the man it represents would have been a priest to the temple's two crocodile gods, Pnepheros and Petesouchos. The priest would have been involved with the daily cult activities of the temple and its periodic festivals, and he may have even been involved in oracles delivered by the crocodile gods or the mummification of actual crocodiles as votive offerings.

The Kelsey Museum statue has a number of parallels from elsewhere in the Fayum region, and a similar statue from Soknopaiou Nesos very closely resembles this example (Bianchi 1992). Most of these statues are inscribed, some in Greek and some in Egyptian Demotic, and the Kelsey statue would have had an inscription on its base when finished. The figure itself was left unfinished: minor detailing work was not done and the base and back pillar are rough, in preparation for a text that was never inscribed. Therefore, we do not know the name of our Karanis priest and can only guess about the specifics of his titles and duties from what is known generally about priests of his time.

1. Statue of a Priest
Black basalt; 50.5 cm h., 18 cm w., 29.5 cm l.
AD 50–100
Karanis, Egypt; University of Michigan Excavation, 1928, Field number 28-SG-QIII, 27-SG-BVI
KM 8218
Bibliography: Bothmer 1960, 50–51; Gazda 1978, 41–42 (no. 35); Bianchi 1992

Karanis: Early History

The village of Karanis was established in the mid-3rd century BC as part of a wider land reclamation effort under Ptolemy II Philadelphos (284–246 BC) (fig. 23). Karanis was one of many such settlements founded in the Fayum at this time: existing irrigation systems were substantially revamped to increase available farmland. The Ptolemaic government moved settlers into the Fayum, many of them soldiers and administrators, and granted land for them to farm, and the overall culture of the town showed varying degrees of Hellenization. Both Greek and Egyptian languages were used, but Greek dominated as the language of administration and business. The religious life of Karanis accommodated both Egyptian and Greek gods and cults, and there was considerable overlap and amalgamation. Much of what we know of the early history of Karanis comes from papyri: frustratingly little artifactual material from this early period was recovered in the Michigan excavations, leaving many uncertainties about the early stages and growth of Ptolemaic Karanis.

Fig. 23. Head of a Ptolemaic king (possibly Ptolemy IV) found at Karanis (KM 8513).

2

2. Anthology with summaries and quotations of *Iliad* XVIII–XIX
Papyrus, ink; 11.5 cm w., 8.6 cm h.
Later Ptolemaic period (ca. 150–30 BC)
Karanis, Egypt; University of Michigan Excavation, 1926 (P.Mich.inv. 4832c), Field number 26-B13F-A
Courtesy of the University of Michigan Library Papyrus Collection
Bibliography: Renner 1979, 331–337; Cribiore 1996, 259 (no. 345)

A wide range of Greek literature was found at Karanis, reflecting a diverse literary culture. This papyrus is a school text, in which an advanced student has summarized portions of Homer's *Illiad*, interspersed with quotations from the text.

3. Lamp in the form of a standing man
Clay; 2.8 cm h., 4.9 cm w., 8.8 cm l.
1st century BC–1st century AD
Karanis, Egypt; University of Michigan Excavation, 1929, Field number 30-C137*-S

KM 22220
Bibliography: Shier 1978, 55 (no. 11)

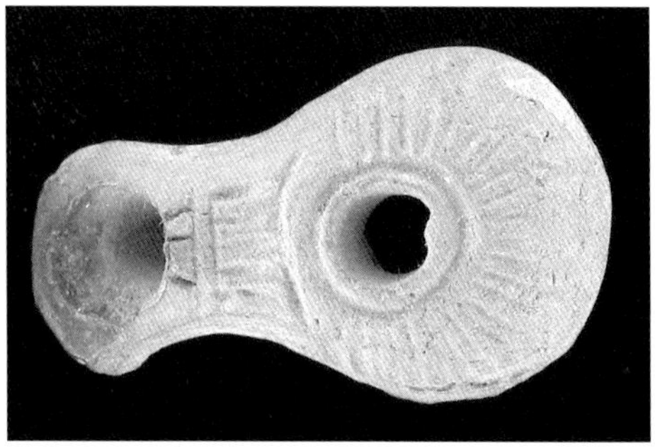
5

4. Lamp
Clay; 3.2 cm h., 6.3 cm w., 10.1 cm l.
1st century BC–1st century AD
Karanis, Egypt; University of Michigan Excavation, 1929,
Field number 29-C137B-B
KM 22195
Bibliography: Shier 1978, 59 (no. 29)

5. Miniature lamp
Clay; 1.6 cm h., 2.1 cm w., 3.6 cm l.
1st century BC–1st century AD
Karanis, Egypt; University of Michigan Excavation, 1929, Field number 30-C137*-HI
KM 22213
Bibliography: Shier 1978, 63 (no. 47)

6. Three-spouted lamp
Clay; 4 cm h., 7.7 cm w., 9.7 cm l.
1st century BC–1st century AD
Karanis, Egypt; University of Michigan Excavation, 1929, Field number 29-C137A-QI
KM 22226
Bibliography: Shier 1978, 69 (no. 79)

Note: All of these lamps are from house C137 at Karanis, which seems to preserve material from the later Ptolemaic period. Certainly the forms of the lamps reflect a Ptolemaic date.

7. Statue base with fragment of hieroglyphic inscription
Limestone; 3.1 cm h., 5 cm w., 6.8 cm l.
2nd–1st century BC
Karanis, Egypt; University of Michigan Excavation, surface find
KM 25758
Bibliography: Unpublished

7

8

Translation: An offering which the king gives to Osiris. May he give invocation offerings of bread, beer, meat, and fowl for the soul of [. . .

Egyptian language material from Karanis is much less common than Greek, but some inscriptions in hieroglyphs, such as this one, and papyrus fragments in hieratic and Demotic scripts were uncovered by the Michigan excavation.

8. Relief showing the god Serapis
Limestone; 3.5 cm h., 8.6 cm w., 14 cm l.
1st–3rd century AD
Karanis, Egypt; University of Michigan Excavation, 1927, Field number 27-C57H-Q
KM 8214
Bibliography: Haeckl and Spelman 1977, 56–57 (no. 41); Gazda 1978, 38–39 (no. 30)

The Egyptian god Serapis shows the complex uses and adaptations of indigenous religion in response to the arrival of Greek traders and settlers in Egypt. The Egyptian hybrid deity Osiris-Apis was further Hellenized to correspond to Greek Zeus, resulting in the god Serapis, who was very popular among Egyptians, Greeks, and Romans in Egypt.

9

9. Coin of Ptolemy II Philadelphos
Obverse: Head of Ammon; Reverse: Eagle on thunderbolt
Bronze; 1.7 cm dia., 0.2 th., 3 g
271–270 BC
Karanis, Egypt; University of Michigan Excavation, surface find
KM 40096
Bibliography: Haatvedt and Peterson 1964, 99 (no. 1)

10. Coin (tetradrachm) of Cleopatra VII, minted at Paphos
Obverse: Head of Ptolemy I Soter; Reverse: Eagle on thunderbolt
Silver; 2.5 dia., 0.4 th., 12 g
37 BC
Karanis, Egypt; University of Michigan Excavation, 1930, surface find, Field number 30-SG-UIII
KM 40369
Bibliography: Haatvedt and Peterson 1964, 105 (no. 47)

11. Coin of Augustus Caesar
Obverse: Head of Augustus; Reverse: Eagle on thunderbolt
Bronze; 1.9 cm dia., 0.3 cm th., 4 g
30 BC–AD 14
Karanis, Egypt; University of Michigan Excavation, surface find
KM 40389
Bibliography: Haatvedt and Peterson 1964, 106 (no. 53)

12–16. "Barbarous" coins of the indigenous rebellion under Ptolemy X
Bronze; 1.8–2.0 cm dia., 0.25–0.35 cm th., 4–5 g

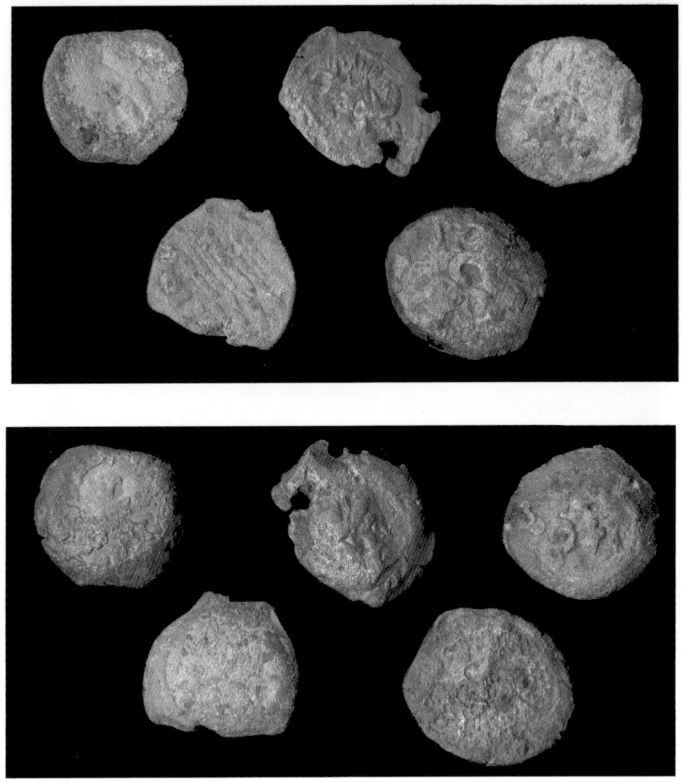

12–16

86–84 BC
Karanis, Egypt; University of Michigan Excavation, 1926 and 1929, Field number 26-B44A-E (KM 40373), 29-C137A-MIII (KM 40374), 29-C137A-MIII (KM 40375), 29-E3E-D (KM 40376) and 1929 surface find (KM 40377)
Bibliography: Haatvedt and Peterson 1964, 106 (no. 51)

Coins are the most secure evidence of the earlier history of Karanis, although Ptolemaic coins are much less common than later coins at the site. Ptolemaic coins even attest to political disturbance: the fact that coins issued by indigenous rebels against Ptolemy X reached the then small village of Karanis suggests how far the repercussions of this rebellion might have reached. Many of the Ptolemaic coins from the site are surface finds—from destruction debris or material dredged up from earlier levels through more recent construction.

Religion at Karanis: Egyptian and Hellenistic Traditions

Religion was a major part of the lives of the inhabitants of Karanis. It featured prominently in both private and public life, with the Michigan excavation unearthing two temples and a wide variety of household devotional objects and shrines. As Greek traders and settlers came into Egypt, Greek religion became a part of Egyptian life, and the material from Karanis shows both Egyptian and Greek gods being worshipped simultaneously. There were also amalgamations of existing deities, such as Isis-Aphordite and, one of the most popular gods at Karanis, Serapis.

At Karanis specifically, forms of the Egyptian crocodile-headed god Sobek (Suchos in Greek) were very popular: Petesouchos and Pnephoros were the primary crocodile gods revered in the South Temple. In some of the ceremonies conducted by the cult priests, mummified crocodiles were brought out for display upon the high altar of the temple. Another god whose cult was popular in the village, particularly during the Roman period, was Harpocrates (a Greek rendering of the Egyptian for Horus-the-Child—fig. 24). He represented the fertility of the land and protected children; he was often associated with Serapis and Isis, forming a divine triad. Traditional Egyptian gods, such as Bes, Anubis, and Osiris, continued to play important parts in religion at Karanis well into the Roman period.

Fig. 24 Mural of the child god Harpocrates and the sphinx god Tutu, from Karanis house C65. Watercolor facsimile by Hamza Carr, 1925 (KM 2003.2.1).

17

17. Falcon-headed crocodile statue of the god Soknopaios
Limestone; 15.5 cm h., 10.2 cm w., 28 cm l.
1st century BC–1st century AD
Karanis, Egypt; University of Michigan Excavation, 1924, surface find
KM 25752
Bibliography: Gazda 1978, 39 (no. 31)

18. Amulet: Head of Serapis
Wood; 3.5 cm h., 8.6 cm w., 14 cm l.
1st–2nd century AD
Karanis, Egypt; University of Michigan Excavation, 1929, Field number 29-B179P-F
KM 8512
Bibliography: Unpublished

19. Figure of Isis-Aphrodite
Ceramic; 7.1 cm h., 2.2 cm w., 1.5 cm l.
1st–3rd century AD
Karanis, Egypt; University of Michigan Excavation, 1928, Field number 28-B168K-U
KM 6488
Bibliography: Gazda 1978, 74 (no. 83); Allen 1985, 2:406–407 (no. 78)

18

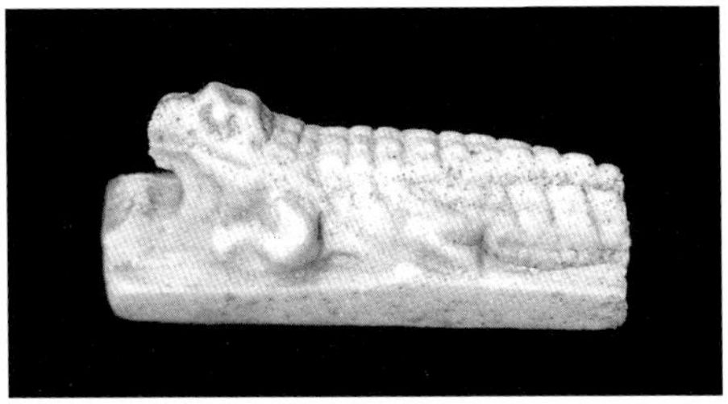

21

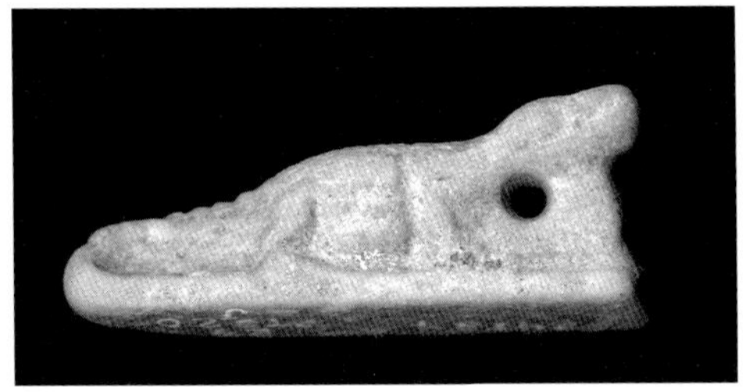

22

20. Ostrakon with image of a crocodile god in a shrine
Clay, ink; 9.8 cm w., 7.4 cm h.
1st–3rd century AD
Egypt, Fayum region; Askren Purchase, 1925 (O.Mich.inv. 4270 = O.Mich. I 97)
Courtesy of the University of Michigan Library Papyrus Collection
Bibliography: Amundsen 1935, 97 and pl. 2; Gazda 2004, 34, fig. 58

21. Crocodile amulet
Faience; 0.5 cm h., 0.4 cm w., 1.5 cm l.
1st century BC–1st century AD
Karanis, Egypt; University of Michigan Excavation, 1928, Field number 28-C85K-A
KM 6285
Bibliography: Unpublished

22. Crocodile amulet
Faience; 0.7 cm w., 3.1 cm l.
1st century BC–1st century AD
Karanis, Egypt; University of Michigan Excavation, 1929, Field number 29-TS20-J
KM 24184
Bibliography: Unpublished

Crocodile gods were especially popular throughout the Fayum in the Graeco-Roman period, with many local variations on the original crocodile god Sobek (Suchos in Greek).

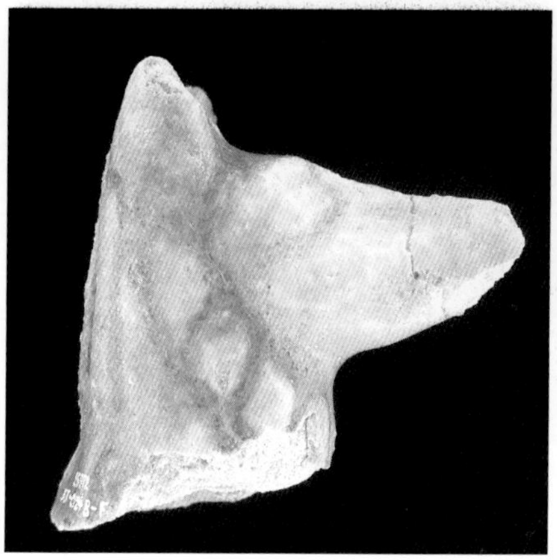

23

24

26

23. Head of jackal: Anubis
Faience; 4.4 cm h., 3.8 cm w., 7.3 cm l.
1st century BC–1st century AD
Karanis, Egypt; University of Michigan Excavation, 1933, Field number 33-C124B-F
KM 25972
Bibliography: Unpublished

In addition to the major crocodile gods, Karanis was also home to a cult of the jackal-headed funerary god Anubis (Rübsam 1974, 98).

24. Figure of Bes
Faience; 8.03 cm h., 4.9 cm w., 2.6 cm l.
1st–3rd century AD
Karanis, Egypt; University of Michigan Excavation, surface find
KM 25979
Bibliography: Unpublished

Amulets of Bes are perhaps the most commonly encountered images of indigenous Egyptian gods at Karanis.

25. Figure of lion
Limestone; 6.2 cm h., 6.7 cm w., 7.8 cm l.
2nd–4th century AD
Karanis, Egypt; University of Michigan Excavation, 1930, Field number 30-B227*-D
KM 25783
Bibliography: Gazda 1978, 27 (no. 11)

26. Ostrakon with an image of a god (Osiris?) in a shrine
Clay, ink; 0.7 cm h., 12.7 cm w., 12 cm l.
2nd–3rd century AD
Karanis, Egypt; University of Michigan Excavation, 1926, Field number 26-B5H-V
KM 93002
Bibliography: Unpublished.

27. Figure of Osiris as a mummy
Ceramic; 21.5 cm h., 6.7 w., 4 cm l.
1st century BC–1st century AD
Karanis, Egypt; University of Michigan Excavation, 1929, Field number 29-E44A-A
KM 6479
Bibliography: Gazda 1978, 74 (no. 90); Allen 1985, 2:384–385 (no. 65, incorrectly cited as KM 6579)

Found in Context

The Michigan expedition uncovered more than 68,000 individual objects at Karanis in its eleven-year duration (1924–1935), and many of these objects were found together—both unintentional accumulations in rooms and deliberate assemblages stored or hidden. The context of the Karanis artifacts is an important part of their value to scholarship. The relations among objects and the places where they were found and the things they were found with all add enormously to our understanding of this ancient site.

These objects were found together in house 216 (fig. 25), along with other pottery vessels and baskets that stayed in Egypt. Seen in isolation, these pieces can be appreciated as works of art or utilitarian objects. The painted pottery shows something of Karanis inhabitants' appreciation for decoration and animal motifs, while the basket and wooden stamp seal show varying levels of craft.

But, found as they were, dumped together on the floor of a house from Karanis's later period of occupation, they attest to the overall activities and property of a household of the 4th–5th centuries AD. The circumstances of their finding also suggest their ultimate value: however beautiful or useful they may have been, in the end their owners decided they were not worth taking away when they abandoned the house.

Fig. 25. Pottery, basketry, and other items as found in house 216 (Kelsey Museum neg. no. 5.2831). Note that this house was excavated in two phases in 1925 and 1927.

28

29

28. Jar with animal and bird motifs (showing ibex)
Painted pottery; 24.7 cm h., 21 cm dia.
3rd–5th century AD
Karanis, Egypt; University of Michigan Excavation, 1925, Field number 25-216C-K
KM 7967
Bibliography: Drawing of design: Johnson 1981, cover; Maguire et al. 1989, 122–123 (no. 54)

29. Mixing bowl with designs
Painted pottery; 20.5 cm h., 31.5 cm rim dia.
3rd–5th century AD
Karanis, Egypt; University of Michigan Excavation, 1927, Field number 27-216A-d
KM 20731
Bibliography: Unpublished

30. Basket with handles
Palm leaf; 16.5 cm h., 28.5 cm w., 13 cm l.
3rd–5th century AD

30

32

Karanis, Egypt; University of Michigan Excavation, 1927, Field number 27-216A-C
KM 8530
Bibliography: Unpublished

31. Stamp
Wood; 3.6 cm h., 6.3–6.5 cm dia.
3rd–5th century AD
Karanis, Egypt; University of Michigan Excavation, 1927, Field number 27-216A-D
KM 24661
Bibliography: Unpublished

32. Jar
Painted pottery; 12 cm h., 8 cm rim dia., 9 cm shoulder dia.
3rd–5th century AD
Karanis, Egypt; University of Michigan Excavation, 1925, Field number 25-216C-i
KM 20216
Bibliography: Unpublished

Fragments

In storage, the Kelsey Museum holds more than 300 plastic bags filled with pieces of broken glass from the Karanis excavation. Far from being a random accumulation, however, this broken glass provides useful information. Each bag preserves the glass from a particular find—usually a specific room in a house or area in a courtyard—and the number and types of glass vessels represented in the fragments can give clues about the activities of a house and the relative status of its inhabitants. The glass fragments shown as object **33** were found together in a rubbish dump near houses of the later periods of the town's habitation. Matching diagnostic pieces—fragments that preserve a rim or a base, for example—to complete examples of similar vessels helps to reconstruct the contents of this find.

Complete or near-complete glass vessels from Karanis tend to come from deliberate caches, often protectively hidden in wooden boxes or large pottery storage vessels known as pithoi. Glass vessels were treated as valuable objects: carefully stored, mended when possible, and reused once their original function was no longer practical. Most of the complete glass vessels found by the Michigan excavation were abandoned by their owners—in some cases left sitting against walls but in others carefully stored away, possibly with the intention to reclaim them on some future return to the site that never took place.

33. Fragments of many vessels found in area 5048
Glass
3rd–4th century AD

33

Karanis, Egypt; University of Michigan Excavation, 1924, Field number 24-5048-AQ
KM 5827
Bibliography: Individual fragments published in Harden 1936, 89 (no. 199), 202 (nos. 559–560), 215 (no. 636), 217 (no. 652), 273 (no. 806), 278 (no. 839), 293 (no. 908), 294 (no. 929)

These fragments were all found together in an area that may have been a courtyard later used as a dump. Many kinds of glass vessels and objects are represented among these fragments, which often preserve features such as rims, handles, or bases that permit reconstruction of the original size and form of the vessels. The objects that follow are complete examples of the kinds of vessels represented in this find of fragments.

34. Perfume bottle (unguentarium)
Glass; 10 cm h., 4.8 cm base dia.
2nd–4th century AD
Karanis, Egypt; University of Michigan Excavation, 1932, Field number 32-C63M-B
KM 6297
Bibliography: Unpublished

35. Perfume bottle (unguentarium)
Glass; 15.5 cm h., 2.8 cm rim dia., 1.4 cm shoulder dia., 2.7 cm base dia.
2nd–4th century AD
Karanis, Egypt; University of Michigan Excavation, 1934, Field number 32-288-VI
KM 6329
Bibliography: Unpublished

36. Bowl
Glass; 5.5 cm h., 14 cm rim dia., 6–6.5 cm base dia.
3rd–4th century AD
Karanis, Egypt; University of Michigan Excavation, 1925, Field number 25-209C-H
KM 5525
Bibliography: Harden 1936, 76 (no. 113)

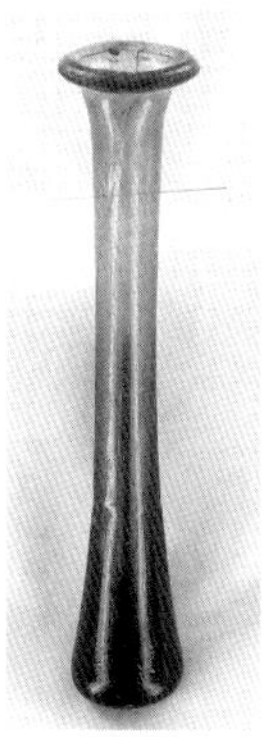

35

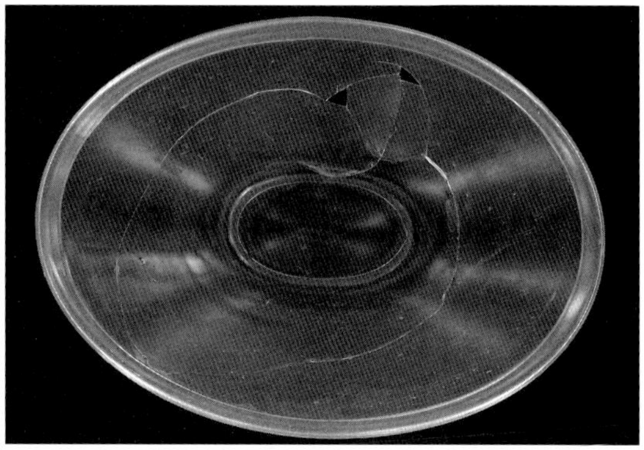

38

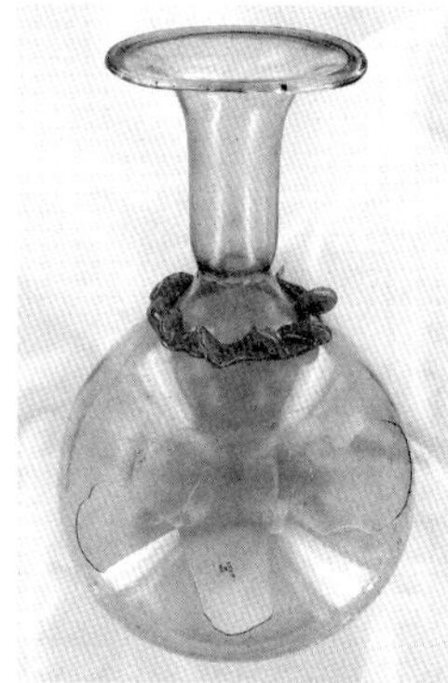

39

37. Bowl
Glass; 4.5–5.5 cm h., 16–16.5 cm rim dia., 77.5 cm base dia.
3rd–4th century AD
Karanis, Egypt; University of Michigan Excavation, 1925, Field number 25-209C-N
KM 5526
Bibliography: Harden 1936, 76 (no. 114)

These two bowls were found with several other similar bowls, carefully stored in a large clay pot in house 209.

38. Oval dish
Glass; 5.5 cm h., 17.5 cm w., 24.5 cm l.
3rd–4th century AD
Karanis, Egypt; University of Michigan Excavation, 1924, Field number 24-133I-A
KM 5684
Bibliography: Harden 1936, 52 (no. 2)

This dish was found in the fill above the floor of house 113, room I, along with several coins of the early 4th century AD.

39. Wine flask
Glass; 24 cm h., 15.25 cm w.
3rd–4th century AD

Karanis, Egypt; University of Michigan Excavation, 1928, Field number 28-C42F-A
KM 5937
Bibliography: Harden 1936, 198 (no. 534)

This flask was found leaning against the wall of house C42, room F, along with many other glass vessels.

Occupations and Activities at Karanis

Agriculture was the primary activity of Karanis, and indeed for the whole of Egypt. Throughout the village's history, its main crop was wheat, and its cultivation dictated much in the lives of the villagers. Their yearly routine followed the cycle of agriculture with the flooding of the Nile between June and August, sowing the fields in November, and harvesting the wheat in mid-April. When farmers and their families were not working in the fields, they could maintain personal gardens or earn additional income by hiring themselves out to individuals or institutions in need of extra labor. In addition to wheat, the villagers of Karanis grew other produce, such as olives, dates, and grapes; although labor intensive, some form of garden was maintained by about half of the village inhabitants. Pigeons were also raised as a reliable source of both fertilizer and meat, and many dovecotes survive at Karanis (fig. 26). Besides agriculture and husbandry, the most extensive industry at Karanis was weaving: more than 3,500 textiles were recovered during the excavations. Cloth and garments were produced for personal use, trade, and tax (in AD 310–301, for example, the village paid 24 tunics to the Roman government for use in the army). A wide range of craft activities at Karanis is seen in surviving tools and the resulting crafted objects.

Fig. 26. A view of the eastern sides of the dovecote C65, showing jars for pigeon nests (Kelsey Museum neg. no. 5.3489).

41

42

40. Bow drill
Wood, iron, bronze; 33 cm dia., 45 cm l., 12 cm spike l.
3rd–4th century AD
Karanis, Egypt; University of Michigan Excavation, 1925, Field number 25-232A-G
KM 3741
Bibliography: Unpublished

41. Miniature hammer
Wood; 2.8 cm h., 6.1 cm w., 12 cm l.
3rd–4th century AD
Karanis, Egypt; University of Michigan Excavation, 1925, Field number 25-5048-KI
KM 3774
Bibliography: Unpublished

42. Agricultural toggle
Wood, palm fiber; 20 cm w., 2.5 cm dia., extended full length of cord 91 cm l.
3rd–4th century AD
Karanis, Egypt; University of Michigan Excavation, 1924, Field number 24-124E-A
KM 8256
Bibliography: Unpublished

43. Loom weight
Unfired clay, string; 4.5 cm h., 8 cm dia.
2nd–4th century AD
Karanis, Egypt; University of Michigan Excavation, 1924, Field number 24-xxi-A
KM 10052
Bibliography: Unpublished

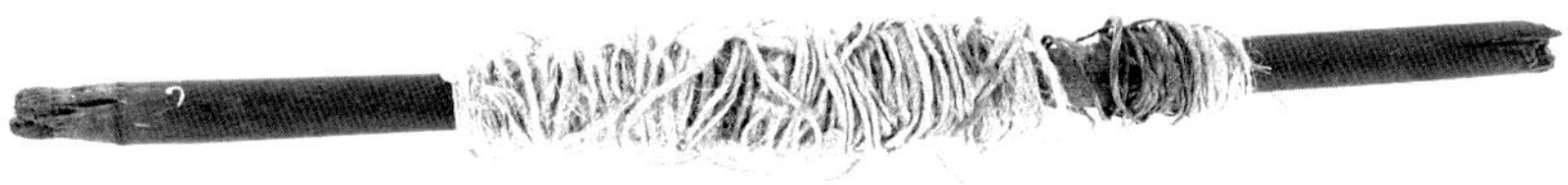

45

47

44. Spindle whorl
Wood; 4.2 cm whorl h., 6.4 cm dia., 9 mm spindle dia., 17 cm l.
2nd–4th century AD
Karanis, Egypt; University of Michigan Excavation, 1924, Field number 24-101J-E
KM 3800
Bibliography: Unpublished

45. Spindle with thread
Reed, cotton; reed 12.3 cm l.
3rd–4th century AD
Karanis, Egypt; University of Michigan Excavation, 1925, surface find
KM 3646
Bibliography: Kelsey Museum 1980, 25 (no. 30)

46. Knitted sock fragment
Wool; 15.5 cm l., 10.0 cm w.
3rd–4th century AD
Karanis, Egypt; University of Michigan Excavation, 1928, Field number 28-209*-C
KM 94655
Bibliography: Unpublished

47. Grape knife
Wood, iron; 4 cm h., 12.7 cm w., 12 cm l.
2nd–4th century AD
Karanis, Egypt; University of Michigan Excavation, surface find
KM 1986.7.1
Bibliography: Unpublished

48. Cake of fuel or animal fodder
Olive pressings; dimensions variable
2nd–4th century AD
Karanis, Egypt; University of Michigan Excavation, 1924, Field number 24-169Q-B
KM 4797
Bibliography: Unpublished

In 1996 Dr. Delwyn Samuel determined that this material, thought by the original excavators to be bread, was instead the remains of crushed olive pits and olive skins, residue from the manufacture of olive oil.

Money, Taxes, Agriculture, and Paperwork

Following the victory of Augustus at Actium in 31 BC, Egypt was incorporated into the wider Roman Empire, and with that came new laws and a more extensive tax system. The Romans instituted levies on a wide variety of commodities, such as beer, salt, and manure, and on occupations. While taxes on property were often paid in grain—which was gathered up in local granaries (fig. 27) by the *sitologi* (superintendent) and eventually shipped to Rome—many of the new duties were paid in coin (fig. 28). By the late 3rd century AD, taxes were required to be settled in gold, so officials would gather the various payments in kind and bronze before selling the whole sum in order to obtain the necessary gold. This complex process generated an enormous amount of paperwork, with village tax lists, receipts for payments made, complaints of embezzlement and overtaxation, etc. Such bureaucratic documents and related material form the majority of the papyri and ostraka discovered by the Michigan excavation at Karanis.

Fig. 27. View of granary C123 from northwest (Kelsey Museum neg. no. 5.3831).

Fig. 28. Coins from a Karanis hoard: Hoard 16, found in a cloth bag in structure B501, room G (KM 66998–67110).

49. Tax register from Karanis, column 19
Papyrus, ink; 30 cm h., 21.2 cm w.
AD 173–174
Egypt, Karanis, Purchase 1924 (P.Mich.inv. 4172, col. 19 = P.Mich. IV 225)
Courtesy of the University of Michigan Library Papyrus Collection
Bibliography: Youtie et al. 1936–1939

This section of papyrus is part of a much longer roll recording the daily collection of money taxes in the village of Karanis in AD 173–174. This column covers collection of taxes on three days in mid-February 174 from named men, including a few slaves. Entries for the day's collections conclude with an overall total. Although taxation was always a fact of life in ancient Egypt, the Roman period saw the introduction of many new taxes and a complex system for their collection.

50. Coin (aureus) from Karanis Hoard 4: reign of Antoninus Pius
Obverse: Head of Antoninus Pius; Reverse: Victory
Gold; 1.85 cm dia., 0.3 cm th., 7.33 g
AD 156–157
Karanis, Egypt; University of Michigan Excavation, 1926, Field number 26-B11L-A
KM 41002
Bibliography: Haatvedt and Peterson 1964, 156 (no. 386)

51. Coin (aureus) from Karanis Hoard 4: reign of Antoninus Pius
Obverse: Head of Antoninus Pius; Reverse: Victory
Gold; 1.9 cm dia., 0.3 cm th., 7.31 g
AD 156–157
Karanis, Egypt; University of Michigan Excavation, 1926, Field number 26-B11L-A
KM 41003
Bibliography: Haatvedt and Peterson 1964, 156 (no. 387)

These gold coins were part of a hoard of 60 coins of similar date found in a cloth bag in house B11, room L. They represent an enormous accumulation of wealth and may even have been the stolen proceeds of tax collections, stashed but never recovered.

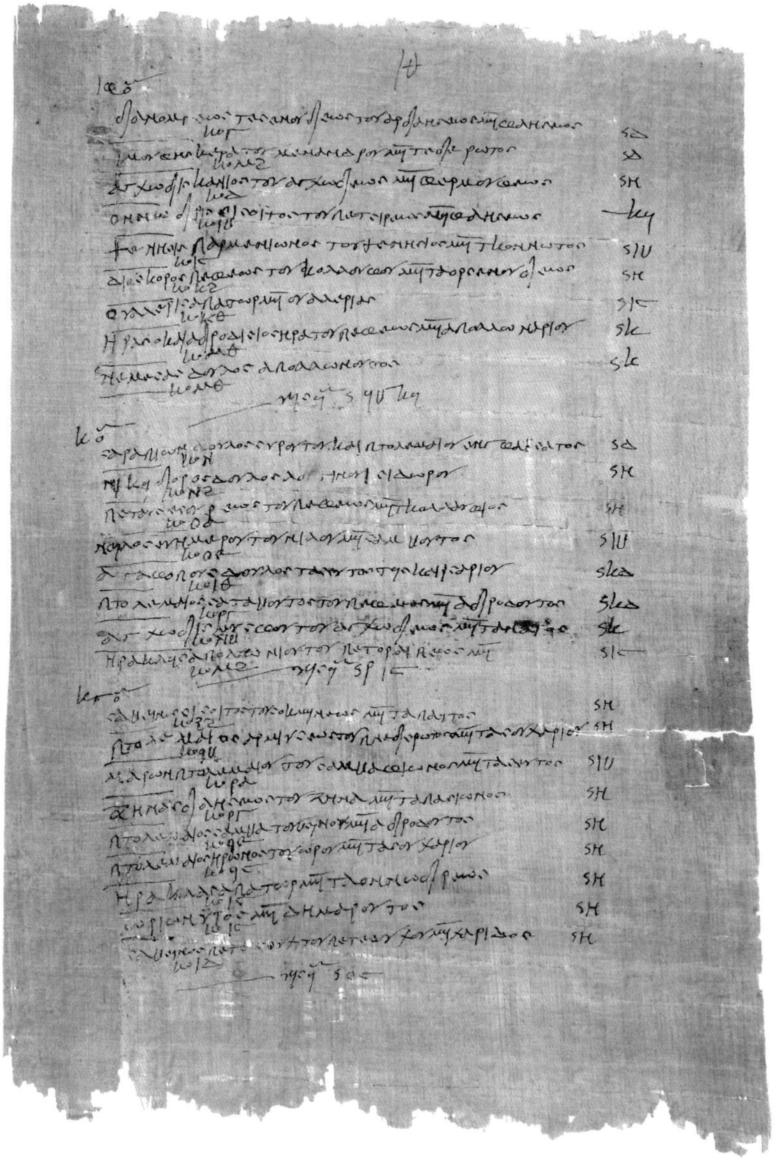

54

52. Grain scoop
Wood, iron; 6 cm h., 25.5 cm w., 32 cm l.
2nd–3rd century AD
Karanis, Egypt; University of Michigan Excavation, 1924, Field number 24-4018-B
KM 3355
Bibliography: Gazda 2004, 10, fig. 16

53. Winnowing fork
Wood; 8 cm h., 24.5 cm w., 30.5 cm l.
3rd–4th century AD
Karanis, Egypt; University of Michigan Excavation, 1924, Field number 24-5020G-B
KM 3420
Bibliography: Gazda 2004, 10, fig. 16

54. Wheat
3rd–4th century
Karanis, Egypt; University of Michigan Excavation, 1924, Field number 24-116C/D-A
KM 3958
Bibliography: Unpublished

Although many other crops were grown by Karanis inhabitants and many other industries practiced there, the activities of the village of Karanis were centered, first and foremost, on wheat: its growth, harvest, storage, processing, and distribution.

Lost, Discarded, and Hidden

Stray earrings, single coins: many of the thousands of objects found at Karanis are clearly items accidentally lost by their owners. Other items, such as worn-out clothing, torn sandals, and broken glass, were obviously discarded when they were unusable. Karanis inhabitants were thrifty, however, and their threshold for what was "unusable" was fairly high by modern standards: clothing was darned and patched, metal objects mended, papyri erased and reinscribed, and even broken pottery vessels were repurposed as writing material in the form of ostraka.

Other objects found at Karanis show definite signs of being deliberately hidden: a hoard of 60 gold coins found in a bag, luxurious bronze objects buried in a large pottery storage jar, and personal items carefully wrapped in cloth and stored in a tiny wooden box are just a few examples. Some objects from the later levels of the site seem clearly to have been stashed with the intention of coming back for them, but these hidden objects seem ultimately to have been forgotten or intentionally abandoned.

Fig. 29. Small rectangular wooden box containing items hidden inside, as found (Kelsey Museum neg. no. 5.1385).

55

56

55. Coin (aureus) from Karanis Hoard 4: reign of Antoninus Pius
Obverse: Head of Antoninus Pius; Reverse: Victory
Gold; 1.9 cm dia., 0.3 cm th., 7.28 g
AD 156/157
Karanis, Egypt; University of Michigan Excavation, 1926, Field number 26-B11L-A
KM 41004
Bibliography: Haatvedt and Peterson 1964, 156 (no. 387)

56. Coin (solidus) of Valens
Obverse: Bust of Valens; Reverse: Valens standing, holding globe surmounted by Victory
Gold; 1.7 cm dia., 3 g
AD 364–378
Karanis, Egypt; University of Michigan Excavation, surface find
KM 65279
Bibliography: Haatvedt and Peterson 1964, 330 (no 1537)

57. Pair of earrings, found together
Gold, glass; 1.2 cm wire l., 1 cm stone l.
2nd–4th century AD
Karanis, Egypt; University of Michigan Excavation, 1927, Field number 27-C56J-A
KM 23007-8
Bibliography: Unpublished

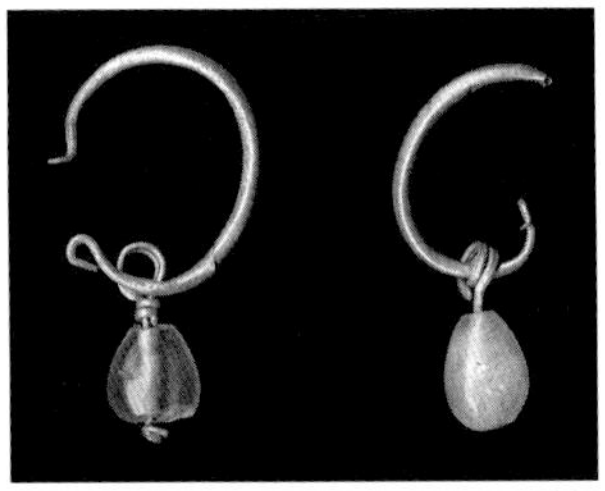

57

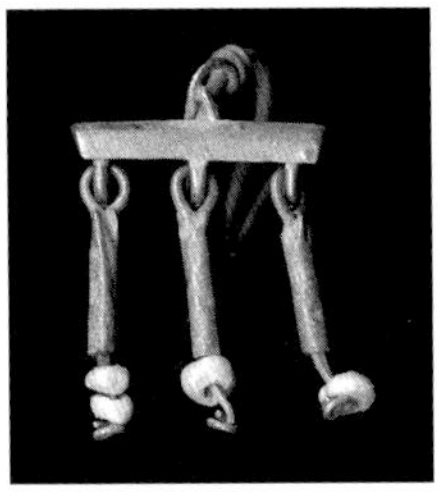

58

59

58. Single earring
Gold, pearls; 2.6 cm h., 1.5 cm w.
2nd–4th century AD
Karanis, Egypt; University of Michigan Excavation, 1928, Field number 28-C108D-E
KM 1999.2.1
Bibliography: Unpublished

59. Necklace of beads found together
Glass, 1.2 cm h., 1.2 cm dia., 49 g
2nd–4th century AD
Karanis, Egypt; University of Michigan Excavation, surface find
KM 78821
Bibliography: Unpublished

Home Security

The clay seal was by far the commonest security device in ancient Egypt, used for doors, storage boxes, jars, and documents: a lump of wet clay was stamped with a seal and allowed to dry. The resulting seal impression would not prevent tampering but would show whether something had been tampered with.

The Ptolemaic period saw the introduction of locks into Egypt, and these became common in the Roman period. These simple pin locks, worked with a wooden or metal key, required the use of two hands—one to operate the key and the other to slide out the released bolt (fig. 30). Such locks were used on some doors and storage boxes, although clay seals continued in use for documents and jars.

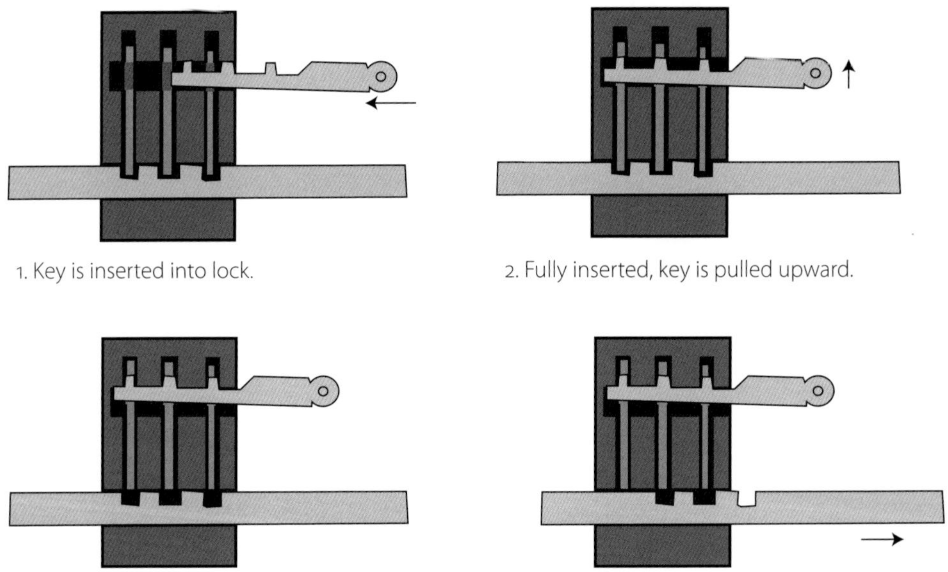

1. Key is inserted into lock.

2. Fully inserted, key is pulled upward.

3. Key raises the three pins and releases the door bolt.

4. Door bolt can now slide out of hole in doorjamb.

Fig. 30. Diagram showing operation of Karanis door lock (drawing by author, based on object **64**).

60. Lock case
Wood, iron; 5.5 cm h., 10.5 cm w., 25.3 cm l.
3rd–4th century AD
Karanis, Egypt; University of Michigan Excavation, 1925, Field number 25-

60

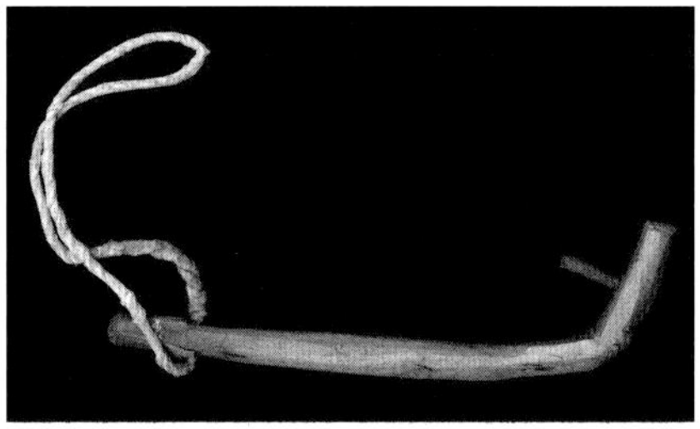

61

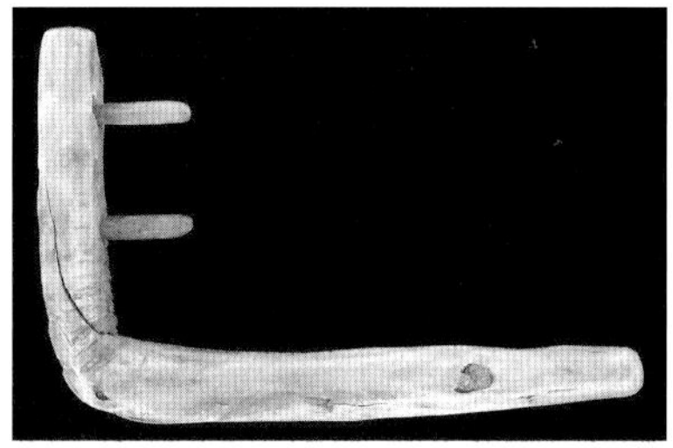

62

4016-G
KM 3516
Bibliography: Unpublished

61. Key with original "keychain"
Wood, string; 2.1 cm h., 6 cm w., 21.1 cm l., 17 cm string l.
3rd–4th century AD
Karanis, Egypt; University of Michigan Excavation, 1924, Field number 24-159E-B
KM 3349
Bibliography: Unpublished

62. Key
Wood; 2 cm h., 9.5 cm w., 14.5 cm l.
3rd–4th century AD
Karanis, Egypt; University of Michigan Excavation, 1925, Field number 25-307G-A
KM 3865
Bibliography: Unpublished

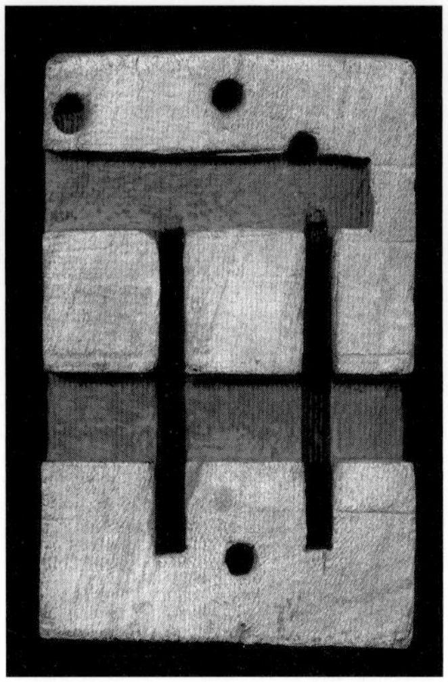

63

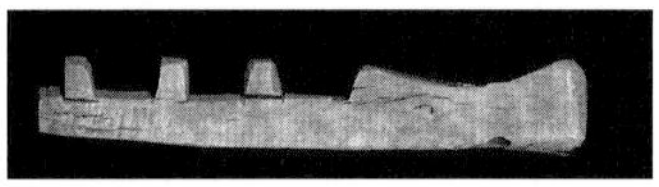

65

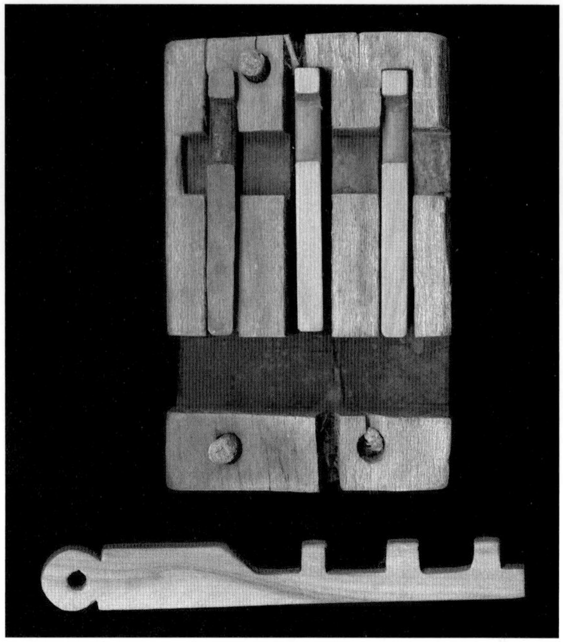

64

63. Lock case
Wood; 3.3 cm h., 10.3 cm w., 15.4 cm l.
3rd–4th century AD
Karanis, Egypt; University of Michigan Excavation, 1924, Field number 24-146B-A
KM 3342
Bibliography: Unpublished

64. Lock case with replica key and restored pins
Wood; 4.3 cm h., 8.7 cm w., 13.6 cm l.
3rd–4th century AD, with modern restored parts
Karanis, Egypt; University of Michigan Excavation, 1929, Field number 29-C88D-A
KM 10238
Bibliography: Gazda 2004, 24, fig. 38

65. Key
Wood; 1.0 cm h., 2.3 cm w., 14.3 cm l.
3rd–4th century AD
Karanis, Egypt; University of Michigan Excavation, 1924, Field number 24-169AE^2-A
KM 3347
Bibliography: Unpublished

66. Windowpane?
Mica; 1.6 cm h., 13.4 cm w., 27 cm l.
1st–4th century AD
Karanis, Egypt; University of Michigan Excavation, surface find
KM 26979
Bibliography: Unpublished

67–69. Seal impressions showing the Egyptian god Serapis
Unbaked clay; 1.2 cm th., 3.5 cm dia.
2nd–3rd century AD
Karanis, Egypt; University of Michigan Excavation, 1930, Field number 30-C123CCH1-E
KM 24430-24432
Bibliography: Unpublished; edition in preparation by Jennifer Gates-Foster

All of these seal impressions, and many others, come from the granary C123, for which see the article by Jennifer Gates-Foster below, pp. 143–148.

67–69

Karanis Stratigraphy

The site of Karanis presents a complex layering that archaeologists call stratigraphy, thanks to more than 700 years of new houses being built on top of old ones. The original excavators of Karanis identified five layers of major construction at the site, to which they assigned dates based on the presence of dated artifacts (especially coins and papyri) and other evidence (fig. 31):

Top level or level A: ca. AD 300–450
Level B: ca. AD 200–300
Level C: ca. AD 50–200 (with three sublevels)
Levels D, E, and F: ca. 250 BC–AD 50

This interpretation of the layering, or stratigraphy, of the site has shaped all subsequent understanding of the archaeology of Karanis.

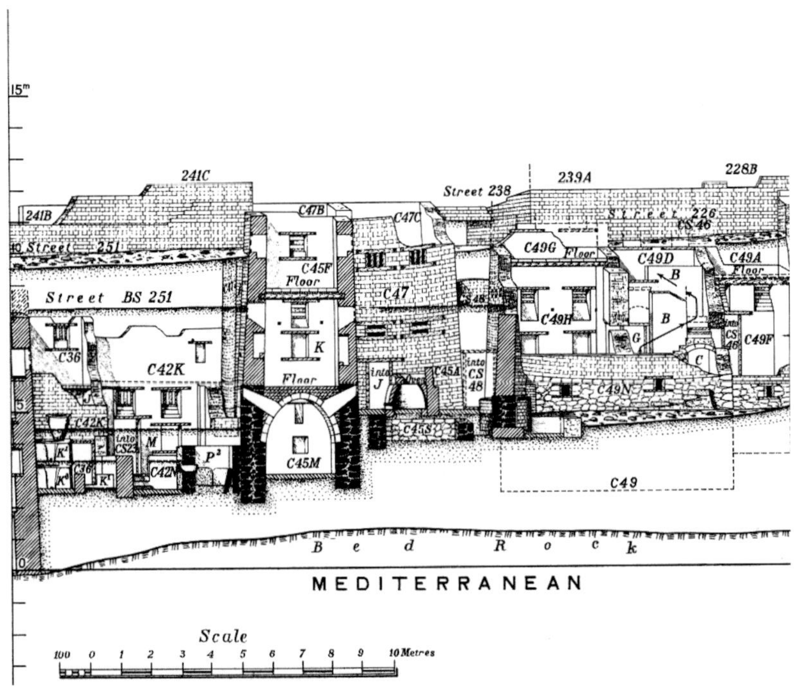

Fig. 31. This sample of a stratigraphic sectional plan of Karanis shows the original excavators' identification of the levels in the site: North-south section through square F10-G10 (adapted from Kelsey Museum neg. no. M8.1511).

The identification of layers and the dates assigned to them were always understood as approximate and to some extent provisional, and more recent research (including work by University of Michigan alumnus Thomas Landvatter, for which see his article above on pp. 39–43) shows the stratigraphy of Karanis to be much more complex than originally envisioned. The original excavators relied most often on the explicitly dated artifacts, such as papyri, ostraka, and coins, that have tended to trump other kinds of evidence in the dating of structures and levels at Karanis. But the disposition of such material in the site can be problematic, and their use for dating structures and layers at Karanis needs to take into consideration the circumstances of their deposition and their relations to other kinds of evidence.

Also, newer research is suggesting that the final abandonment of Karanis was later than the mid-5th-century AD date proposed by the original excavators—with habitation extending at least sporadically into the 6th and perhaps even 7th century. New excavations at Karanis will doubtless result in further changes to our understanding of the complex stratigraphy of the site.

Finding Magic at Karanis

Many forms of magic were practiced in the ancient world—for healing, love, power, control, and other purposes—and ancient magical practice often left traces in the archaeological record. Written magical texts and spells are the most direct form of evidence, but drawings and objects made, worn, modified, destroyed, and deposited in the course of magical rituals can also attest to acts of magic. The Karanis excavations yielded much material that could be related to magic: archaeologist and University of Michigan alumnus Andrew Wilburn analyzed material from Karanis and other sites throughout the Roman world to identify and understand the archaeological evidence of magical practice, and also to arrive at a wider theoretical approach to such material (see article below, pp. 153–156).

Some evidence for magic at Karanis is fairly straightforward: magical spells on papyrus and magical amulets proclaim their magical nature outright, although their archaeological context can sometimes provide subtler clues as to the use of such textual material. More often, however, the evidence for magic at Karanis comes with some ambiguity. A tiny pierced and burned figure of a woman is almost certainly magical in nature, part of a spell of "love" or erotic compulsion. But the precise details of its ritual use and ultimate intent are harder to decode.

Other objects are even more ambiguous, and the temptation for the archaeologist is to assume that anything odd or unusual is "magical" in nature, without a more careful analysis. The sketch of a naked woman on a potsherd has no obvious purpose, and it could be part of an erotic magical ritual: its emphasis on the sexual features of the figure and the adjoining image of an altar or flower may support this idea. But the precise function of such a magical figure is unclear, and the drawing may have been made for another, nonmagical purpose.

70. Amulet on bracelet
Lead, string
3rd–4th century AD
Karanis, Egypt; University of Michigan Excavation, 1928, Field number 28-165*-P
KM 24255
Bibliography: Wilburn 2012, 130–131.

Lead was commonly used for magical texts in the ancient world, often for curses,

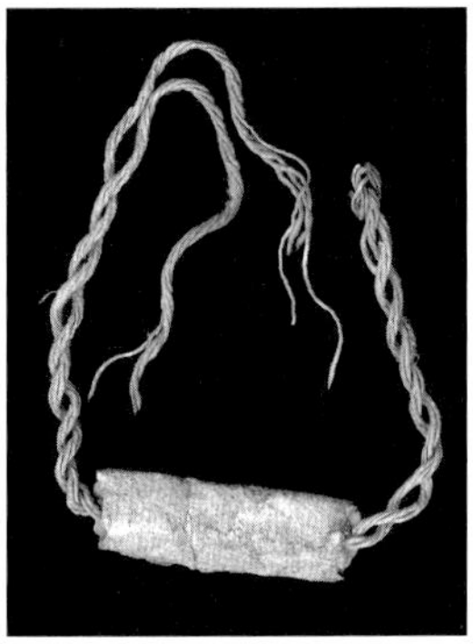

70

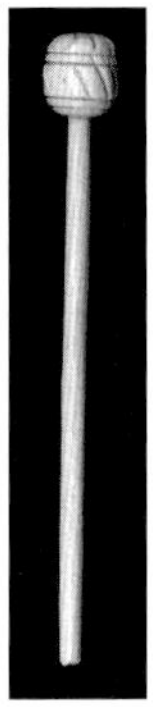

71

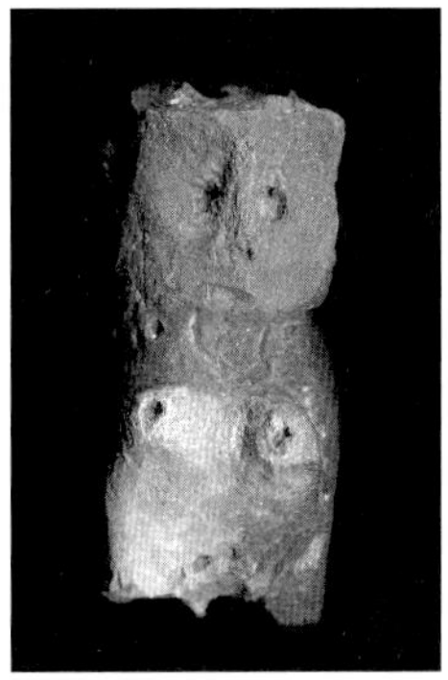

72

but in this case the strip of lead would probably have been inscribed with a protective magical text before being wrapped around the string and worn as a bracelet. The size suggests the amulet and bracelet were intended for a child. The lead has never been unwrapped, so the text inscribed on it is still a mystery.

71. Hairpin
Bone
3rd–4th century AD
Karanis, Egypt; University of Michigan Excavation, 1928, Field number 28-165*-CII
KM 21776
Bibliography: Wilburn 2012, 132.

72. Figurine of a woman
Clay
3rd–4th century AD
Karanis, Egypt; University of Michigan Excavation, 1928, Field number 28-165*-WII
KM 7525
Bibliography: Wilburn 2012, 131–139

This clay figurine of a woman was probably burned in a magical ritual, perhaps a love spell. The bone hairpin, found with the figurine, may have been used to pierce the holes used to indicate features, and may also have been a possession of the woman on whom the spell was being cast.

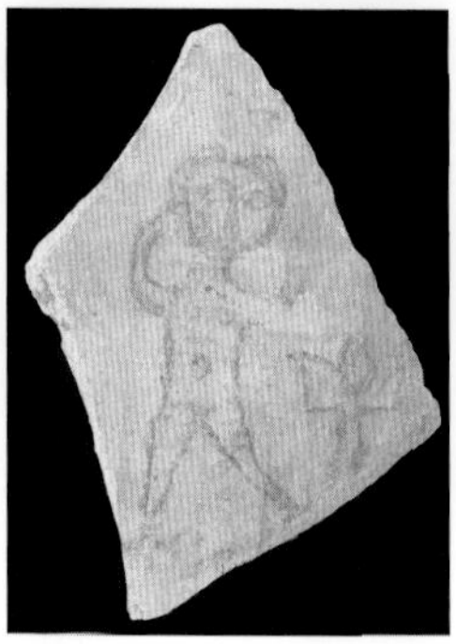

73

73. Ostrakon with drawing of a woman
Clay, ink
3rd–4th century AD
Karanis, Egypt; University of Michigan Excavation, 1924, Field number 24-5006A-AD
KM 92999
*Bibliography:*Wilfong 1997, 76 (no. 71)

Sometimes the original intent of objects from Karanis remains obscure. This ostrakon is one of a number of ostraka from Karanis bearing drawings of uncertain intent. This drawing could simply be an artist's sketch but is perhaps more likely to have been intended for magical purposes.

74. Fever amulet
Papyrus, ink; 10 cm w., 7.5 cm h.
4th century AD
Karanis, Egypt; University of Michigan Excavation, 1928 (P.Mich.inv. 5302a = P.Mich. XVIII 768), Field number 28-242*-P
Courtesy of the University of Michigan Library Papyrus Collection
Bibliography: Brashear 1996; Wilburn 2012, 109–117

An amulet found at Karanis consisting of invocations of Biblical and magical names and words as a protection against fever. Translation (from the Advanced Papyrological Information System at http://www.lib.umich.edu/papyrus-collection/):

> Iao, Sabaoth, Adonai! I beseech Anatiel, Raphael, Gabriel, Suriel, Azariel, Uriel, . . . aubrael, Ablanathanalba, Sesengembarpharanges. These are the Potentates of God and (the) Powers of the cure. Cure Sarapion, whom Allous bore, from every three-day fever-chill, every-other-day (fever-chill), quotidian (fever-chill) and from every sickness every day(?) . . .

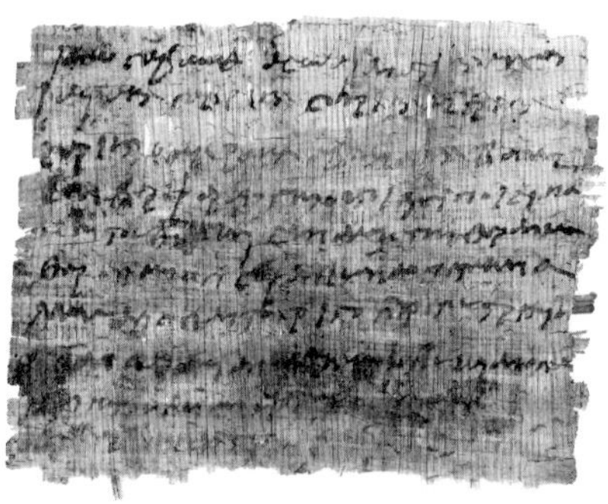

74

Toys in Context

Objects found together at Karanis raise all kinds of questions about their relationships. Clusters of similar objects raise expectations of significance: groups of toys found together (such as the wooden toys in fig. 32) suggest the presence of children in a household, while an assemblage of musical instrument fragments found in the room of a house might imply that the house belonged to musicians. It is tempting to construct narratives using select material from such finds.

But we must be cautious about doing this: the interpretation of such finds needs to take into account all of the available contextual evidence. The find of toys in house 114, for example, includes a wider range of material—pottery jars and bowls, lamps, textiles, glass, and other wooden objects—that attest to complex activities within the household well beyond the play of children. Indeed, the quantity of toys from this find (several more pieces were found that did not come to Michigan) may suggest another possibility: that the house was a site for domestic manufacture of wooden objects, including toys.

Fig. 32. A group of wooden toy horses as found in house BC72 (Kelsey Museum neg. no. 5.2396).

76

79

81

Objects from a Single Find in House 114, Room D

75. Pitcher
Clay; 9 cm h., 7.3 cm dia.
3rd–5th century AD
Karanis, Egypt; University of Michigan Excavation, 1924, Field number 24-114D-av
KM 7206
Bibliography: Unpublished

76. Oil flask
Clay, rope; 13.7 cm h., 9.7 cm dia.
3rd–5th century AD
Karanis, Egypt; University of Michigan Excavation, 1924, Field number 24-114D-a
KM 7269
Bibliography: Unpublished

77. Fragments of plate
Glass; 5.7 cm base dia., largest fragment 1.3 cm h., 6 cm w., 9 cm l.
3rd–5th century AD
Karanis, Egypt; University of Michigan Excavation, 1924, Field number 24-114D-AI

KM 5422
Bibliography: Unpublished

78. Doll
Wood; 1.3 cm h., 3.8 cm w., 12.5 cm l.
3rd–5th century AD
Karanis, Egypt; University of Michigan Excavation, 1924, Field number 24-114D-AY
KM 10003
Bibliography: Unpublished

79. Doll
Wood; 1.4 cm h., 5 cm w., 15.2 cm l.
3rd–5th century AD
Karanis, Egypt; University of Michigan Excavation, 1924, Field number 24-114D-N
KM 10004
Bibliography: Unpublished

80. Comb
Wood; .07 cm h., 7.5 cm w., 12 cm l.
3rd–5th century AD
Karanis, Egypt; University of Michigan Excavation, 1924, Field number 24-114D-C
KM 10011
Bibliography: Unpublished

81. Cooking pot
Clay; 9.5 cm h., 9.3 cm dia.
3rd–5th century AD
Karanis, Egypt; University of Michigan Excavation, 1924, Field number 24-114D-c
KM 7329
Bibliography: Unpublished

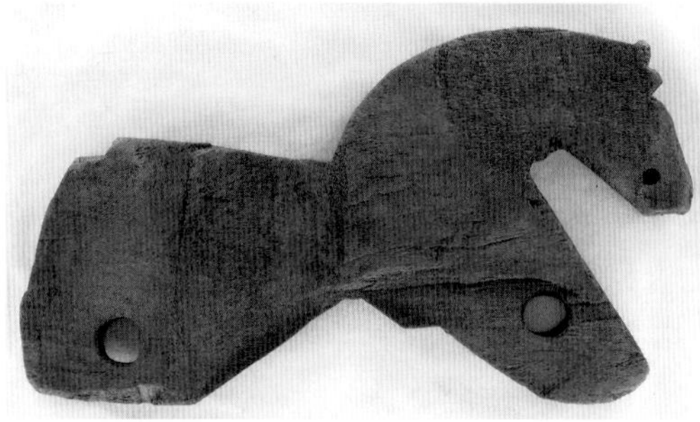

83

88

82. Toy horse body
Wood; 8 cm h., 1.9 cm w., 11.2 cm l.
3rd–5th century AD
Karanis, Egypt; University of Michigan Excavation, 1924, Field number 24-114D-AX
KM 3331
Bibliography: Unpublished

83. Toy horse body
Wood; 9.1 cm h., 1.5 cm w., 17.5 cm l.
3rd–5th century AD
Karanis, Egypt; University of Michigan Excavation, 1924, Field number 24-114D-K
KM 10034
Bibliography: Unpublished

84. Wheel of toy
Wood; 1.3 cm th., 4.4 cm dia.
3rd–5th century AD
Karanis, Egypt; University of Michigan Excavation, 1924, Field number 24-114D-M
KM 10036
Bibliography: Unpublished

85. Wheel of toy
Wood; 1.2 cm th., 5.7 cm dia.
3rd–5th century AD
Karanis, Egypt; University of Michigan Excavation, 1924, Field number 24-114D-M
KM 10040
Bibliography: Unpublished

86. Lamp
Clay; 6.02 cm h., 7.07 cm w., 13 cm l.
3rd–5th century AD
Karanis, Egypt; University of Michigan Excavation, 1924, Field number 24-114D-AQ
KM 22373
Bibliography: Shier 1978, 155 (no. 471)

87. Lamp
Clay; 3.5 cm h., 7 cm w., 12.5 cm l.
3rd–5th century AD
Karanis, Egypt; University of Michigan Excavation, 1924, Field number 24-114D-AU
KM 22345
Bibliography: Shier 1978, 135 (no. 390)

88. Cup
Clay; 6.2 cm h., 8.2 cm w., 9.5 cm l.
3rd–5th century AD
Karanis, Egypt; University of Michigan Excavation, 1924, Field number 24-114D-h
KM 8116
Bibliography: Unpublished

89

89. Cloth fragment
Wool; 11.5 cm w., 20.5 cm l.
3rd–5th century AD
Karanis, Egypt; University of Michigan Excavation, 1924, Field number 24-114D-AH
KM 11355
Bibliography: Unpublished

All of these objects were found together in house 114, room D, in the 1924 season at Karanis. Dated material from the context suggests a 3rd–5th-century AD date for these objects, probably later in that span of time.

Side Project: Dimé (Ancient Soknopaiou Nesos)

In 1931, the Michigan Karanis expedition turned its attentions briefly to the far western Fayum site of Dimé, ancient Soknopaiou Nesos, literally "Island of Soknopaiou" (a crocodile god revered in the Fayum whose name itself means "Sobek, Lord of the Island"). Like Karanis, Soknopaiou Nesos preserved many standing mud-brick houses and yielded large quantities of papyri. Unlike Karanis, Soknopaiou Nesos had a shorter history, having been founded around the same time as Karanis (mid-3rd century BC) but abandoned by the end of the 3rd century AD.

The Michigan team concentrated on two small areas at Soknopaiou Nesos, uncovering part of a large, nonresidential structure that was probably an administrative building along with a group of houses. In addition to artifacts in the Kelsey Museum, the expedition also uncovered substantial quantities of papyri. Notable among these was a small archive of customs-house receipts that attest to the role of Soknopaiou Nesos as a way station for desert trade moving in and out of Egypt (Boak 1935, 23–33).

Dimé was a difficult site for the Michigan team to excavate, especially while maintaining a base at Karanis, and they did not come back to it after the 1931–1932 season. In the subsequent decades, as more and more papyri from Dimé were published, interest in the site increased, and there is now a large-scale effort to excavate Dimé, under the direction of Mario Capasso and Paola Davoli for the University of Lecce (Capasso and Davoli 2012).

90. Lamp
Clay; 2.2 cm h., 5.4 cm w., 8.9 cm l.
1st–3rd century AD
Dimé, Egypt; University of Michigan Excavation, 1931, Field number 31-I 111M-BI
KM 22202
Bibliography: Unpublished

91. Female head from figurine
Clay; 9.9 cm h., 7.3 cm w., 8.6 cm l.
1st–3rd century AD
Dimé, Egypt; University of Michigan Excavation, 1931, Field number 31-II 202F-y

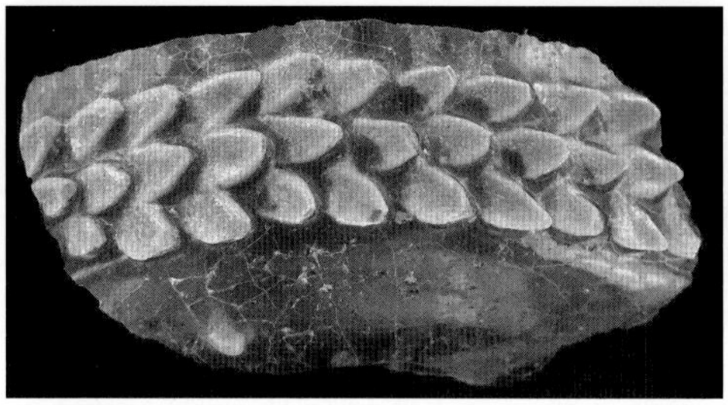
92

KM 6869
Bibliography: Allen 1985, 2:545–547 (no. 137)

92. Fragment of decorated bowl
Faience; 4.7 cm h., 9.6 cm w., 0.9 cm th.
1st–3rd century AD
Dimé, Egypt; University of Michigan Excavation, 1931, Field number 31-I 107K-K
KM 26238
Bibliography: Unpublished

93. Fragment of decorated flask
Glass; 4.8 cm h., 3.4 cm w., 0.2 cm th.
1st–3rd century AD
Dimé, Egypt; University of Michigan Excavation, 1931, Field number 31-II 202F-M
KM 6366
Bibliography: Unpublished

94. Lion figurine
Faience; 3.6 cm h., 3.3 cm w., 1.5 cm l.
1st–3rd century AD
Dimé, Egypt; University of Michigan Excavation, 1931, Field number 31-I 112K-D
KM 25965
Bibliography: Unpublished

94

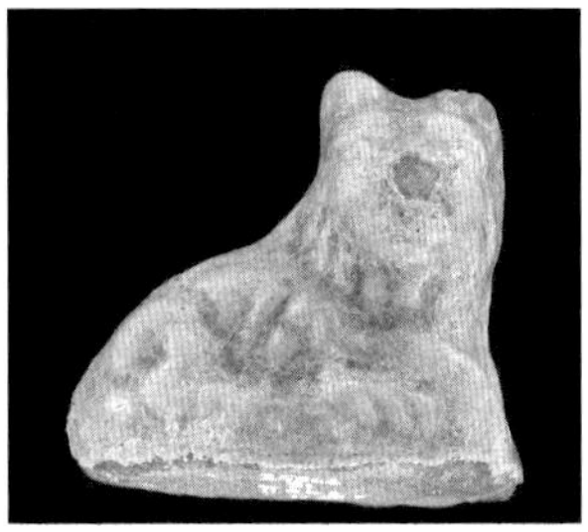

95

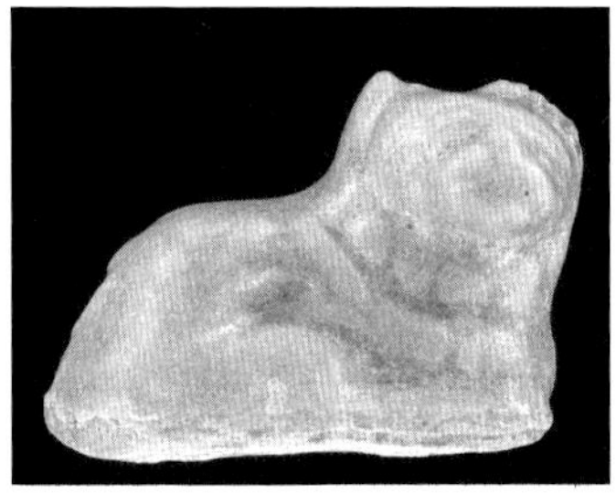

96

95. Lion figurine
Faience; 3.3 cm h., 3.35 cm w., 1.7 cm l.
1st–3rd century AD
Dimé, Egypt; University of Michigan Excavation, 1931, Field number 31-II 202F-HI
KM 25966
Bibliography: Unpublished

96. Lion figurine
Faience; 2.9 cm h., 4 cm w., 1.8 cm l.
1st–3rd century AD
Dimé, Egypt; University of Michigan Excavation, 1931, Field number 31-II 204K-J
KM 25967
Bibliography: Unpublished

97. Textile fragment
Goat hair; 8.5 cm h., 10 cm w.
1st–3rd century AD
Dimé, Egypt; University of Michigan Excavation, 1931, Field number 31-I 110-B
KM 22595
Bibliography: Unpublished

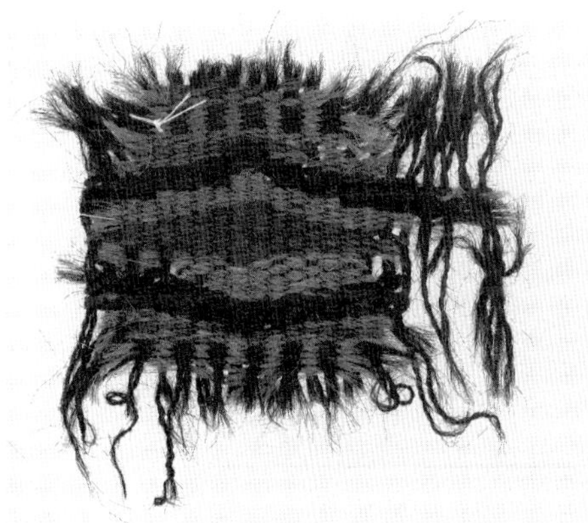

97

98

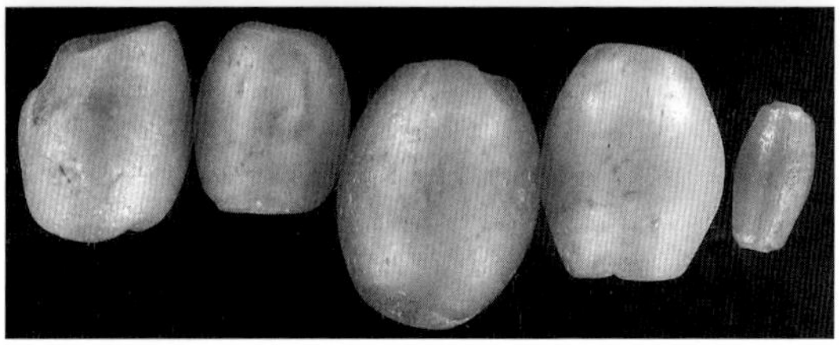

99

98. Beads
Glass; dimensions variable
1st–3rd century AD
Dimé, Egypt; University of Michigan Excavation, 1931, surface find
KM 77747
Bibliography: Unpublished

99. Beads
Glass; dimensions variable
1st–3rd century AD
Dimé, Egypt; University of Michigan Excavation, 1931, surface find
KM 78780
Bibliography: Unpublished

100. Bead
Faience; 1 cm h., 1.6 cm dia.
1st–3rd century AD
Dimé, Egypt; University of Michigan Excavation, 1931, Field number 31-II 202K-LI
KM 77843
Bibliography: Unpublished

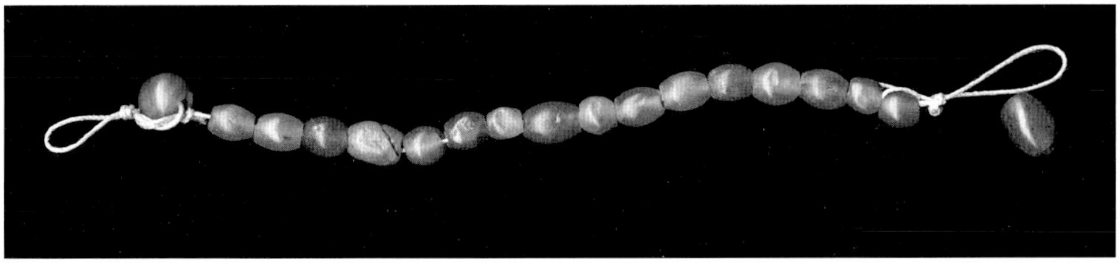

101

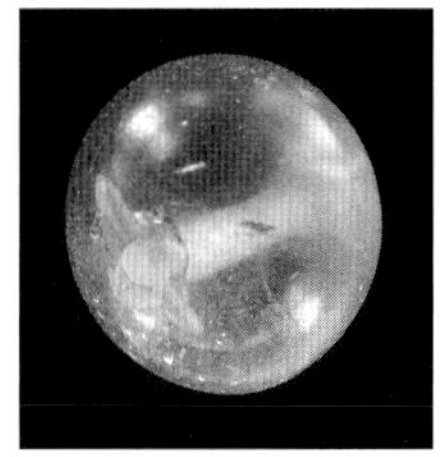

102

101. Beads
Carnelian (on modern string); dimensions variable
1st–3rd century AD
Dimé, Egypt; University of Michigan Excavation, 1931, surface find
KM 78870
Bibliography: Unpublished

102. Bead
Stone (crystal?); 1.5 cm dia.
1st–3rd century AD
Dimé, Egypt; University of Michigan Excavation, 1931, surface find
KM 78899
Bibliography: Unpublished

Side Project: Terenouthis

The cemeteries at Karanis did not yield much in the way of artifactual material, so the Michigan expedition looked elsewhere for material to illustrate mortuary practice in Graeco-Roman Egypt. The western Delta site of Kom Abou Billou, the cemetery of ancient Terenouthis, was chosen to fill this gap, and a month-long test season was undertaken in 1935. The Michigan team found a few burials of the Ptolemaic period, more than 200 funerary stelae from cenotaph shrines of the 2nd century AD (fig. 33) and nearly 200 burials of the later Roman period. Over 2,200 objects were found, most of which subsequently came to Michigan. Recordkeeping for this short season was difficult, and many questions remain about the relations among different groups of material from the excavation. But the Michigan project provided a rare instance of a relatively intact Graeco-Roman period cemetery in Egypt. The Michigan Terenouthis material was the object of a large-scale study in the early 1990s and is now being researched by University of Michigan alumnus Thomas Landvatter.

Fig. 33. Terenouthis grave mound showing placement of funerary stela (Kelsey Museum neg. no. 4.0224).

103. Funerary stela showing a man on a boat
Limestone, paint; 16 cm h., 21 cm w., 4.7 cm th.
2nd century AD
Terenouthis, Egypt; University of Michigan Excavation, 1935, Field number 10-A95
KM 21190
Bibliography: Hooper 1961, no. 191

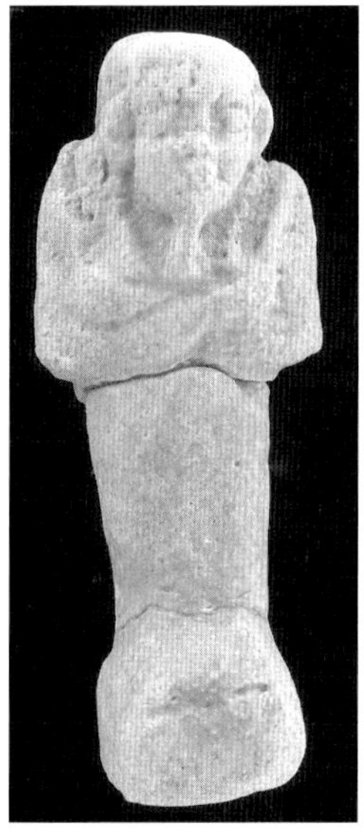
104

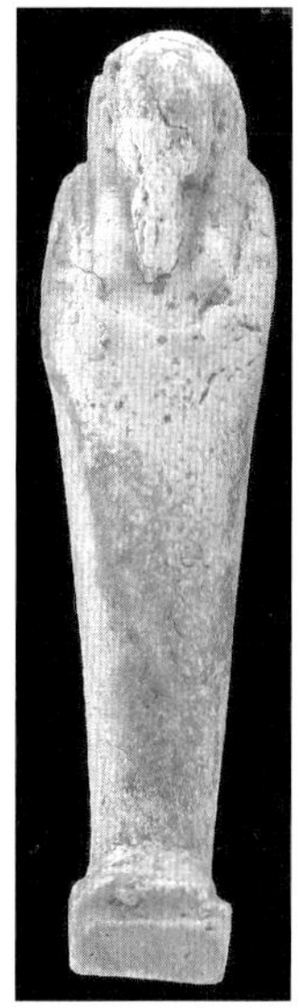
105

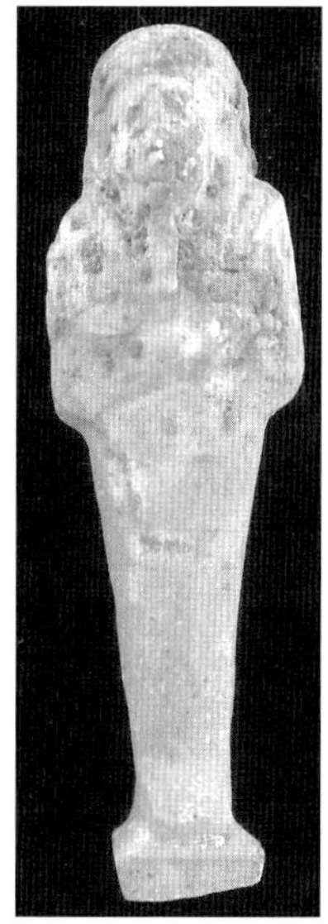
106

104. Shabti figure
Faience; 8.35 cm h., 3.2 cm w., 2.3 cm l.
Ca. 2nd century BC–1st century AD
Terenouthis, Egypt; University of Michigan Excavation, 1935, Field number 3B-A7
KM 92253
Bibliography: Unpublished

105. Shabti figure
Faience; 7.3 cm h., 1.9 cm w., 1.6 cm l.
Ca. 2nd century BC–1st century AD
Terenouthis, Egypt; University of Michigan Excavation, 1935, Field number 3C-A3
KM 92256
Bibliography: Unpublished

106. Shabti figure
Faience; 7.2 cm h., 2.2 cm w., 1.5 cm l.
Ca. 2nd century BC–1st century AD
Terenouthis, Egypt; University of Michigan Excavation, 1935, Field number 3B-A4
KM 92250
Bibliography: Unpublished

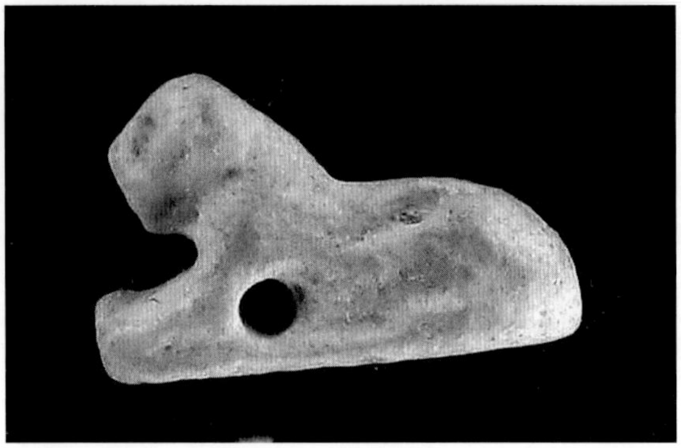

107

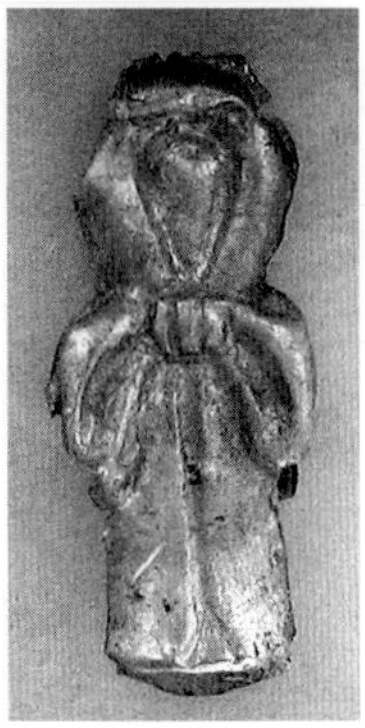

108

107. Lion amulet
Faience; 0.85 cm h., 0.5 cm w., 1.4 cm l.
Ca. 2nd century BC–1st century AD
Terenouthis, Egypt; University of Michigan Excavation, 1935, surface find
KM 24173
Bibliography: Unpublished

108. Isis knot amulet
Gold; 1.4 cm h., 0.6 cm w., 0.1 cm th.
Ca. 2nd century BC–1st century AD
Terenouthis, Egypt; University of Michigan Excavation, 1935, Field number 3C-G2
KM 24222
Bibliography: Unpublished

109. Falcon amulet
Gold; 1.1 cm h., 1.75 cm w., 0.4 cm th.
Ca. 2nd century BC–1st century AD
Terenouthis, Egypt; University of Michigan Excavation, 1935, Field number 3B-B3
KM 24196
Bibliography: Unpublished

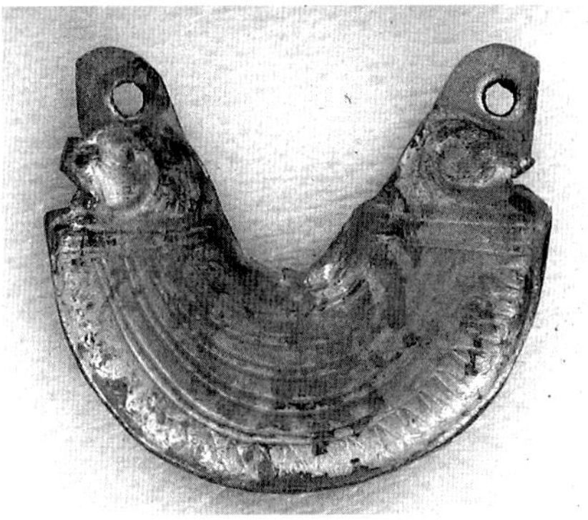

110

110. Broad collar amulet
Gold; 1.7 cm h., 1.9 cm w., 0.15 cm th.
Ca. 2nd century BC–1st century AD
Terenouthis, Egypt; University of Michigan Excavation, 1935, Field number 3C-G3
KM 24224
Bibliography: Unpublished

Late Karanis

Karanis reached the height of its population during the Roman period, having as many as 4,000 inhabitants in the mid-2nd century AD, a time of great prosperity for the Fayum village. Its popularity as a place of settlement for soldiers retiring from military service to a life of agriculture added more inhabitants to the site. The town's prosperity was not to last, however, as plague and economic problems in the late 2nd and 3rd centuries AD resulted in a significant decline (nearly 40 percent) of the community's population. While there was some revival of fortune in the 4th century—as indicated by a variety of coin hoards—the population hovered around 140 landholders, or approximately 700 inhabitants, and never returned to its previous levels. The last securely dated papyrus comes from 15 May 439, in which complaints are made about the scarcity of water, and this has often been cited as the death knell for Karanis. The archaeological record, however, especially the survival of later pottery forms and lamps from the site, and other textual sources point to some sort of habitation into the 6th and possibly 7th century AD (Pollard 1998; Keenan 2003).

111. Canceled receipt
Papyrus, ink; 7.5 cm w, 7.5 cm h.
5th century AD
Karanis, Egypt; University of Michigan Excavation, 1925 (P.Mich.inv. 4604), Field number 25-244-I
Courtesy of the University of Michigan Library Papyrus Collection
Bibliography: Unpublished; edition in preparation by Nikos Litinas and R. James Cook

This papyrus—a receipt for grain—is one of the latest documents to survive from Karanis, dating to sometime between AD 415 and 460. The text is crossed out, a common means of indicating that the receipt has been canceled and was no longer needed. See the discussion of this text on p. 157 below.

112. Coin (tetradrachm) of Galerius, pre-reform of coinage
Obverse: Bust of Galerius; Reverse: Dikaiosyne seated, holding scales and cornucopiae

Billon; 1.9 cm dia., 0.4 cm th., 7.7 g
AD 295/296
Karanis, Egypt; University of Michigan Excavation, 1933, Field number 33-B501J-A
KM 64702
Bibliography: Haatvedt and Peterson 1964, 294 (no. 1402)

113

113. Tetradrachm coins of Galerius, pre-reform of coinage
Obverse: Bust of Galerius; Reverse: Bust of Serapis
Billon; 1.9 cm dia., 0.4 cm th., 7.6 g
AD 295/296
Karanis, Egypt; University of Michigan Excavation, 1933, Field number 33-C418E-C
KM 64716
Bibliography: Haatvedt and Peterson 1964, 295 (no. 1437)

114. Coin (tetradrachm) of Galerius, pre-reform of coinage
Obverse: Bust of Galerius; Reverse: Eagle
Billon; 2.2 cm dia., 0.4 cm th., 8.1 g
AD 295/296
Karanis, Egypt; University of Michigan Excavation, 1933, 33-B501J-A
KM 64719
Bibliography: Haatvedt and Peterson 1964, 295 (no. 1439)

115

115. Coin (tetradrachm) of Diocletian, post-reform of coinage
Obverse: Bust of Diocletian; Reverse: Genius wearing modius
Bronze; 2.6 cm dia., 0.3 cm th., 10.5 g
AD 296–305
Karanis, Egypt; University of Michigan Excavation, 1929, Field number 29-B188A^{8}-A
KM 64744
Bibliography: Haatvedt and Peterson 1964, 298 (no. 1454)

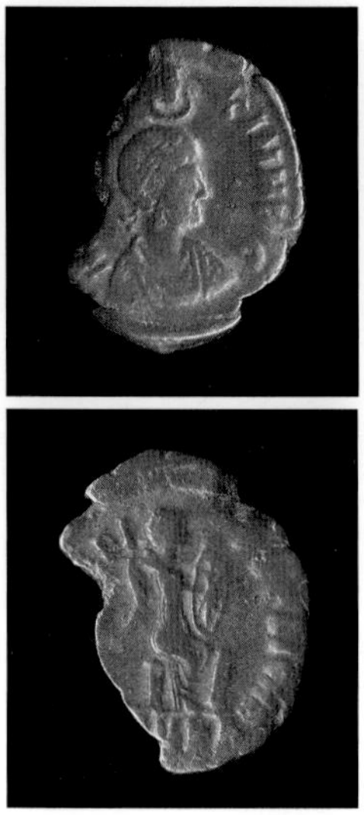

116

116. Coin of Empress Eudoxia
Obverse: Bust of Eudoxia; Reverse: Victory seated
Bronze; 1.0 cm dia., 0.1 cm th., 1.5 g
AD 400
Karanis, Egypt; University of Michigan Excavation, 1925, Field number 24-113D-D
KM 66010
Bibliography: Haatvedt and Peterson 1964, 346 (no. 1734)

117. "Barbarous" coin (minimi)
Obverse: Bust of emperor; Reverse: Inscription in wreath
Bronze; 1.0 cm dia., 0.1 cm th., 0.6 g
4th century AD
Karanis, Egypt; University of Michigan Excavation, 1924, Field number 24-137D-W
KM 66022
Bibliography: Haatvedt and Peterson 1964, 347 (no. 1742)

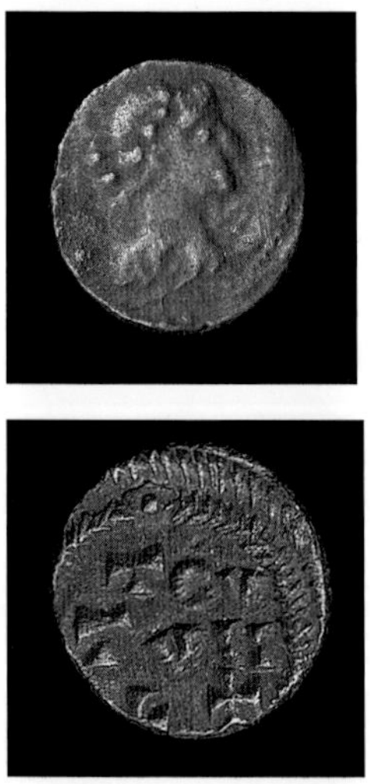

117

118. Coin (10 nummia) of Justinian
Obverse: Bust of Justinian; Reverse: Sign I surmounted by cross
Bronze; 2.2 cm dia., 0.2 cm th., 4.6 g
AD 539/540
Karanis, Egypt; University of Michigan Excavation, surface find
KM 66889
Bibliography: Haatvedt and Peterson 1964, 348 (no. 1744)

119. Coin (12 nummia) of Heraclius
Obverse: Heraclius wearing crown with cross; Reverse: Sign IB, globus with cross
Bronze; 1.9 cm dia., 0.4 cm th., 8 g
AD 610–641
Karanis, Egypt; University of Michigan Excavation, surface find

KM 66890
Bibliography: Haatvedt and Peterson 1964, 348 (no. 1745)

The two latest coins (**118–119**) found in the Karanis excavation show at least some activity at the site in the 6th and 7th centuries, but their status as "surface finds" (found in debris on or near the surface of the site) may suggest that they were dropped by looters, travelers, or traders passing through what was already an abandoned town.

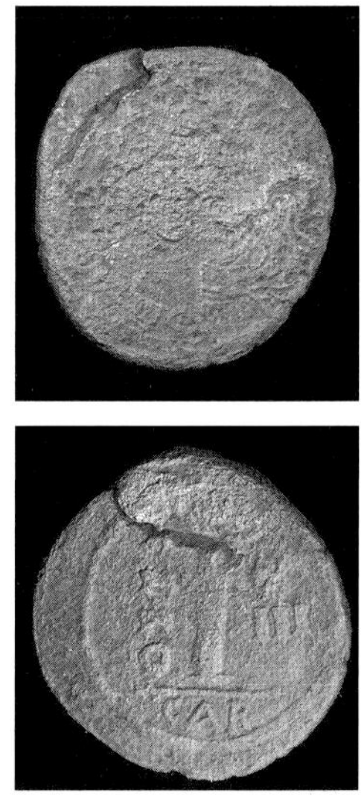

119

120. Textile fragment
Wool, linen; 11 4604 cm h., 8 cm w.
3rd–4th century AD
Karanis, Egypt; University of Michigan Excavation, 1924, Field number 24-5049-H
KM 13127
Bibliography: Wilson 1933, 21–22 (no. 35)

121. Textile fragment with vine leaf design
Wool
3rd–4th century AD
Karanis, Egypt; University of Michigan Excavation, 1924, Field number 24-4034A-G
KM 12249a
Bibliography: Unpublished

121

122. Textile fragment with human figures
Wool, linen; 13 cm h., 10 cm w.
3rd–4th century AD
Karanis, Egypt; University of Michigan Excavation, 1925, Field number 25-191-B
KM 13347
Bibliography: Wilson 1933, 24–25 (no. 52)

123. Lamp with cross decoration
Clay; 6.1 cm h., 8.4 cm w., 14 cm l.
4th–5th century AD
Karanis, Egypt; University of Michigan Excavation, 1927, surface find, Field number 27-SG-Z
KM 22376
Bibliography: Shier 1978, 152 (no. 463)

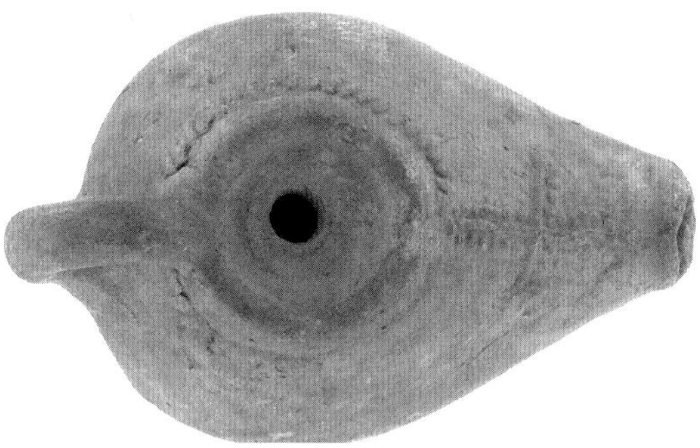

123

Christianity at Karanis

The advent of Christianity marked one of the most significant shifts in Roman Egyptian society. The mechanics of the process, however, remain relatively unclear. Though there is no direct evidence for when Christianity first came to Egypt, by the 3rd century AD, there was a documented Christian population, and pagan temples were beginning to be abandoned. The development of the Coptic script for writing the Egyptian language was contemporary with the rise of Christianity in Egypt and may, in part, have been spurred by it. By the 5th century AD, the majority of Egypt was Christian, with a substantial monastic population and a powerful clerical base in Alexandria.

At Karanis, archaeological evidence for Christianity comes from household contexts rather than any recognizable ecclesiastical institutional structures. These include items such as personal wooden crosses, lamps adorned with Christian symbols, and Biblical texts, like the Coptic fragment of the Book of Job. Though it is known that Karanis had Christian priests (mentioned in a papyrus from AD 439), no archaeological traces of churches have been found. This suggests that such structures may have been in the central portion of the site, destroyed by *sebakh* diggers before the excavation, or that the villagers converted existing pagan temples of Karanis to house their new Christian cult.

124. Fragment of a Biblical codex leaf: the Book of Job in Coptic
Papyrus, ink; 10.5 cm w., 9.1 cm h.
4th–5th century AD
Karanis, Egypt; University of Michigan Excavation, 1928 (P.Mich.inv. 5421), Field number 28-B168L-B
Courtesy of the University of Michigan Library Papyrus Collection
Bibliography: Browne 1979; Kasser and Satzinger 1982

This is a rare, early example of a Coptic Biblical text found in an archaeological context. Irregularities of both script and dialect show that this text was written at a time before Coptic had become fully standardized.

124

125. Seal impressions (used as jar stopper)
Clay; 3 cm h., 4.2 cm w., 6.5 cm l.
2nd–4th century AD
Karanis, Egypt; University of Michigan Excavation, 1924, surface find, Field number 24-X-5
KM 3600
Bibliography: Unpublished

126. Jar stopper with cross
Clay, pigment; 3.9 cm th., 9.4 cm dia.
4th century AD
Karanis, Egypt; University of Michigan Excavation, 1933, Field number 33-BS500-P
KM 29762
Bibliography: Unpublished

Clay stoppers used for sealing jars show crosses and other Christian symbols by the 4th and 5th centuries AD, in patterns not unlike earlier pre-Christian sealings.

127. Lamp with cross design
Clay, pigment; 3.5 cm h., 6.7 cm w., 8.5 cm l.
3rd–4th century AD

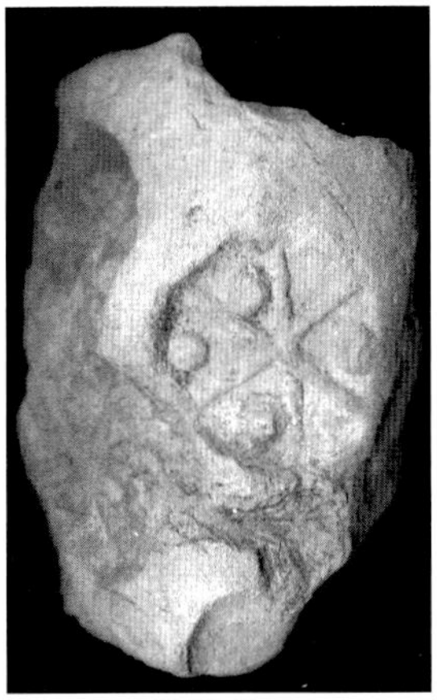

125

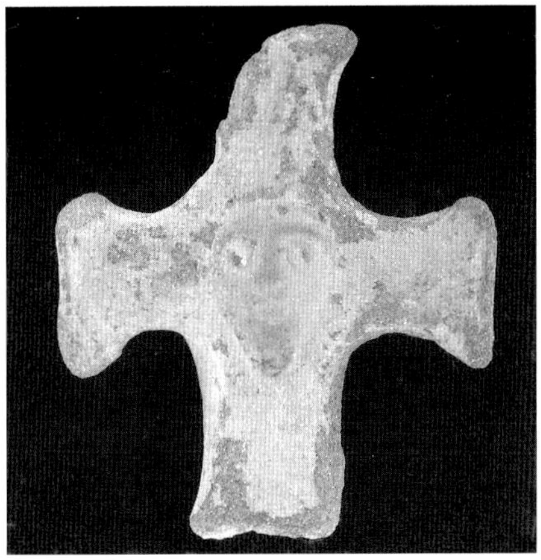

129

Karanis, Egypt; University of Michigan Excavation, 1930, Field number 30-B203K-O
KM 22353
Bibliography: Shier 1978, 141–142 (no. 414)

128. Bowl with stamped decoration of cross
Clay; 6 cm h., 20 cm rim dia., 11 cm base dia.
4th–5th century AD
Karanis, Egypt; University of Michigan Excavation, 1928, Field number 28-C84A-d
KM 7145
Bibliography: Hayes 1972, 153 (Form 99, Type A.5); Johnson 1981, 49 (no. 243); Pollard 1998, 150–151

This reddish pottery, so characteristic of fine wares in Egypt in the later Roman and Byzantine periods, is African Red Slip ware, imported from North Africa and later largely replaced by Egyptian Red Slip ware, made in imitation of the more expensive imports.

129. Cross with human face
Clay, paint; 5.9 cm h., 5.1 cm w., 1.4 cm l.
4th–5th century AD

Karanis, Egypt; University of Michigan Excavation, 1928, surface find
KM 6924
Bibliography: Gazda 1978, 69 (no. 71); Allen 1985, 2:536 (no. 152)

130. Cross pendant
Wood, string; 7.7 cm h., 4.3 cm w., 1.7 cm th.
4th–5th century AD
Karanis, Egypt; University of Michigan Excavation, 1928, Field number 28-165*-AI
KM 7561
Bibliography: Haeckl and Spelman 1977, 101 (no. 109); Gazda 2004, 43 (fig. 75); Maguire et al. 1989, 169 (no. 94)

131

131. Cross pendant
Mother of pearl; 2 cm h., 1.4 cm w., 0.2 cm th.
4th–5th century AD
Karanis, Egypt; University of Michigan Excavation, 1929, Field number 29-B156K*-A
KM 21938
Bibliography: Unpublished

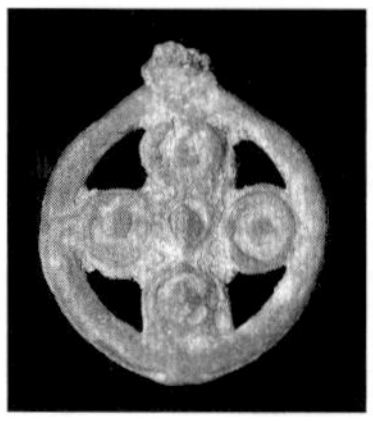
132

132. Cross pendant
Lead; 1.6 cm h., 1.4 cm dia.
4th–5th century AD
Karanis, Egypt; University of Michigan Excavation, 1927, Field number 27-B110F-B
KM 21937
Bibliography: Unpublished

133. Cross pendant
Wood; 4.5 cm h., 2 cm w., 1 cm th.
4th–5th century AD
Karanis, Egypt; University of Michigan Excavation, 1924, Field number 24-71-A
KM 21936
Bibliography: Unpublished

134. Cross pendant
Wood; 5.1 cm h., 3.6 cm w., 1.7 cm th.
4th–5th century AD
Karanis, Egypt; University of Michigan Excavation, 1925, Field number 25-4010C-R
KM 4813
Bibliography: Unpublished

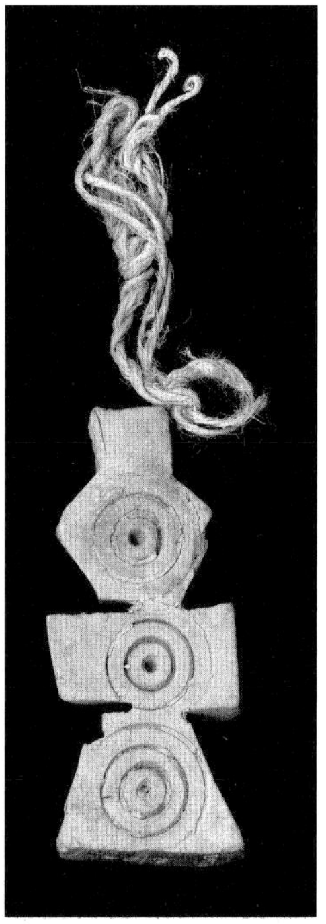

133

134

Fig. 34. Although crosses are often identified as Christian symbols at Karanis, not all Karanis crosses were necessarily Christian, as can be seen in this small phallic cross, probably a good luck or fertility charm, from the Michigan excavations at Karanis (the object was retained by the Egyptian Antiquities Service; Division album photograph, Kelsey Museum neg. no. 542).

Mysterious Bones

Many of the finds at Karanis left the excavators (and subsequent researchers) with questions and puzzles: objects of uncertain purpose abound at Karanis, and the intent behind many assemblages of objects remains unclear. Perhaps no Karanis find is more mysterious than the 105 decorated bones divided between two nearby contexts probably dating to the 4th century AD. These bones—mostly from domesticated mammals like pigs, cows, horses, sheep, and goats but also including a few fish, dog, and even human bones—are painted in red ocher with a variety of dots, lines, and squiggles, some of which slightly resemble writing.

If these bones had been found individually or in small groups, their decoration might have been seen as attempts at writing or even children's scribbles. But the find of these bones in two large groups suggests other possibilities. The use of animal (and human) bones in magical practices of the period, the frequent use of symbols and even "pseudo-writing" in Egyptian magic, and the sheer amount of material strongly suggest to researcher Andrew Wilburn that these bones are a specifically magical deposit. Wilburn's book on the archaeology of magic in the Roman world uses the material from Karanis as an important case study on the various forms of physical evidence for magical practice in the archaeological record.

Another mysterious bone find at Karanis was a pair of sheep horns mounted high in a wall (fig. 35). Whether these were intended for good luck or some other magical purpose, or simply for decoration, is for future scholars to puzzle over.

Fig. 35. Horns set in wall beneath stairway of house C85, Kelsey Museum neg. no. 5.3747).

135. Magical bones: animal and human bones painted with designs
Bone, paint; dimensions variable
3rd–5th century AD
Karanis, Egypt; University of Michigan Excavation, 1925; Field numbers 25-262 and 25-265
KM 3503, 3504, 3535, 10099
Bibliography: Described in Wilburn 2012, 140–160, 284–286; full edition in preparation by Andrew T. Wilburn

135

The Roman Military at Karanis

One of the more exceptional items excavated at Karanis is a piece of leather armor (**138**), found in house 193, room A, which would date it roughly between ca. AD 250 and 350. Though no other specific information can be derived from the archaeological context, much can be read from the armor itself. Its size, quality, and intricacy indicate that it was an expensive item and most likely came from a military context rather than belonging to any local police force. The lightweight leather construction of the armor points to its being equipment for cavalry whose main role was skirmishing, which did not require more extensive protection (fig. 36).

Though the presence of military personnel at Karanis is well documented in the 2nd century, there is little specific information from the late 3rd and early 4th centuries. The best evidence for the Fayum comes from the papyrological records of a cavalry officer stationed in the fort at Dionysias (modern Qasr Qarun), located on the western side of Lake Moeris (fig. 37). Soldiers there were primarily concerned with collecting taxes and often acted as law enforcement. They owned land in several villages across the region and were rarely, if ever, involved in full-scale combat.

Fig. 36. Palmyrene god wearing armor similar to the Karanis fragments (drawing by Lorene Sterner after original statue in the Louvre, ca. AD 50).

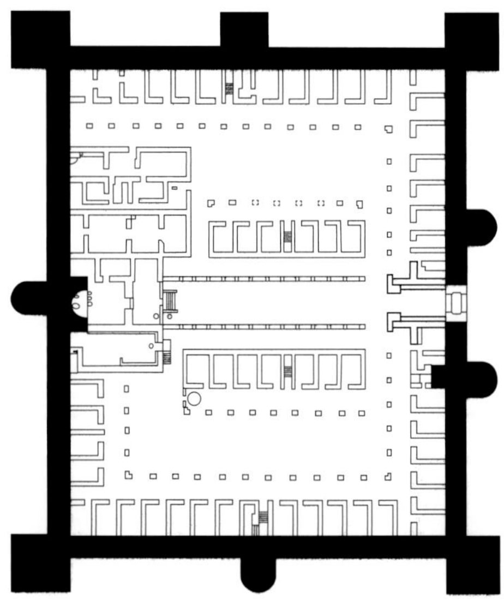

Fig. 37. Plan of Roman fort at Dionysias (drawing by Lorene Sterner after Alston 1995, 205).

136. Ostrakon with drawing of a soldier in armor
Clay, paint; 6.7 cm h., 10.8 cm w., 0.7 cm th.
2nd–3rd century AD
Karanis, Egypt; University of Michigan Excavation, 1925, Field number 28-B166A*-L
KM 7712
Bibliography: Unpublished

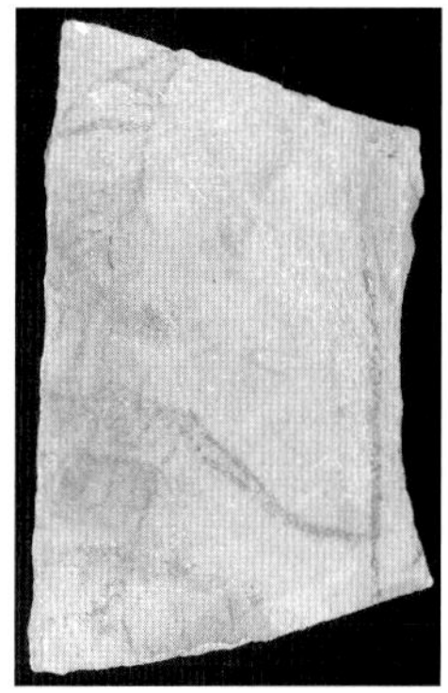

136

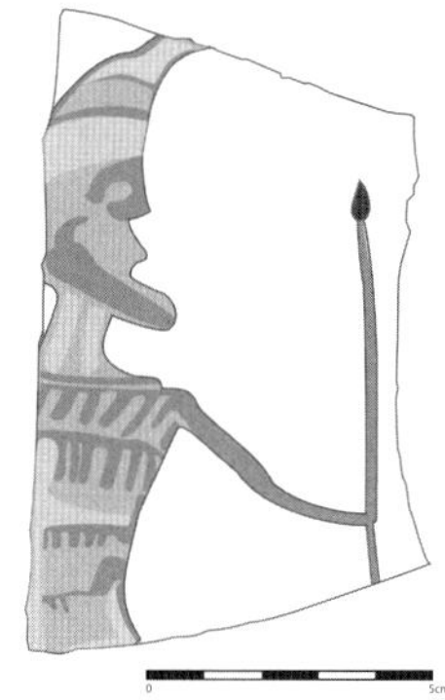

Fig. 38. Drawing of ostrakon by Lorene Sterner.

137. Spear head
Iron, wood; 26.75 cm h., 3.75 cm w.
1st–2nd century AD
Dimé, Egypt; University of Michigan Excavation, 1931, Field number 31-I 108G-B
KM 23120
Bibliography: Unpublished

138. Military armor breastplate (cuirass)
Leather
3rd–4th century AD
Karanis, Egypt; University of Michigan Excavation, 1925, Field number 24-193A-O
KM 3631
Bibliography: Unpublished

This unique piece of leather scale armor from Karanis is discussed in detail in the essays by Andrew Ferrara and Claudia Chemello on pp. 123–139.

Pottery, Everywhere

By far the commonest material for objects from Karanis (indeed from Graeco-Roman Egypt as a whole) was pottery (fig. 39). In addition to the thousands of complete or near-complete pottery vessels and objects brought back to Michigan from Karanis, tens or even hundreds of thousands of broken pieces of pottery were left behind. Pottery was a ubiquitous part of the material culture of Graeco-Roman Egypt—mainly in the form of vessels for the preparation, storage, and consumption of food and drink, as well as lamps for illumination, but also for other portable objects of worship and amusement, and vessels and bins for large-scale storage. Even broken pottery served further purposes as chinking for bricks and mortar, as well as a cheap and convenient writing surface for notations and drawings (known as ostraka).

The pottery from Karanis reflects conventions in the forms and styles of vessels across the Graeco-Roman world. These forms and styles changed over time and can be important clues as to dating. Because of the other contextual information about dating (including dated papyri and coins), the pottery from Karanis can provide valuable material for comparison with pottery from other sites.

Fig 39. A group of objects—mainly pottery—in house 230A (Kelsey Museum neg. no. 5.1802).

139. Wine jar (amphora)
Pottery, slip; 68.6 cm h., 7 cm rim dia., 19 cm shoulder dia.
5th–6th century AD
Karanis, Egypt; University of Michigan Excavation, 1930, surface find, Field number 30-SG-k
KM 20757
Bibliography: Pollard 1998, 155–156.

This amphora is one of a number of later types from the excavation that suggest a later habitation (or subsequent rehabitation) of Karanis beyond the latest known dated document from AD 439.

A Karanis Burial

The Michigan excavation uncovered four burials in the initial 1924 season but did not follow through with formal excavation of the extensive cemeteries near Karanis. Archival photographs document the finding and disposition of the four skeletons now housed in the Kelsey Museum. New research on these remains of individual Karanis inhabitants by researcher Thomas Landvatter reveals much about the hard realities of life at Karanis for individuals in lower economic classes.

This is the skeleton of a woman aged between 55 and 60 years in a burial with no apparent grave goods and no attempt at mummification. The woman's joints show signs of advanced arthritis and of hard physical labor. More striking is the fracture in the woman's left femur (thigh bone). Although entirely healed by the time of her death, this injury left the deceased with a shortened and deformed left leg, to the extent that her movement would have been severely hampered by this disability. Although we do not know her name, careful and respectful study of this woman's remains can provide insight into the conditions of her life at Karanis.

140. Skeleton of a woman
3rd–5th century AD
Karanis, Egypt; University of Michigan Excavation, 1924, Field number Burial 1924.100
KM T2006.3
Bibliography: In situ image published in Wilfong 2012, 241–242; a detailed description of these skeletal remains appears in the essay below by Thomas Landvatter on pp. 141–142.

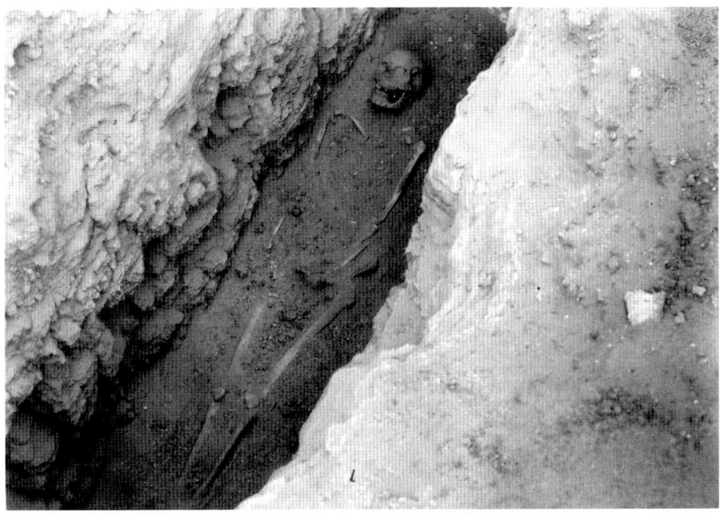

Fig. 40. Skeleton **140** in burial 100, as found by the excavators in 1924 (Kelsey Museum neg. no. 5.1553).

Bibliography

Allen, M. L. 1985. "The Terracotta Figurines from Karanis: A Study of Technique, Style and Chronology in Fayoumic Coroplastics," 3 vols. Ann Arbor: University of Michigan. Ph.D. dissertation.

Alston, R. 1995. *Soldier and Society in Roman Egypt: A Social History*. London: Routledge.

Amundsen, L. 1935. *Greek Ostraca in the University of Michigan Collection: Part I, Texts*. University of Michigan Studies, Humanistic Series, 34. Ann Arbor: University of Michigan Press.

Bianchi, R. S., 1992. "The Cultural Transformation of Egypt as Suggested by a Group of Enthroned Male Figures from the Faiyum." In J. H. Johnson, ed., *Life in a Multi-Cultural Society: Egypt from Cambyses to Constantine and Beyond*. Studies in Ancient Oriental Civilization, 51. Chicago: The Oriental Institute, 15–40.

Boak, A. E. R. 1935. *Soknopaiou Nesos: The University of Michigan Excavation at Dimé, 1931–1932*. University of Michigan Studies, Humanistic Series, 39. Ann Arbor: University of Michigan Press.

Bothmer, B. v. 1960. *Egyptian Sculpture of the Late Period*. Brooklyn: Brooklyn Museum.

Brashear, W. 1996. "768: Fever Amulet." In T. Gagos, and C. Römer, eds., *P.Michigan Koenen (=P.Mich.XVIII): Michigan Texts Published in Honor of Ludwig Koenen*. Amsterdam: Gieben, 75–86.

Browne, G. M. 1979. *Michigan Coptic Texts*. Papyrologica Castroctaviana, 7. Barcelona: Papyrologica Castroctaviana.

Capasso, M., and Davoli, P. 2012. *Soknopaiou Nesos Project I: 2003–2009*. Biblioteca di studi di egittologia e di papirologia, 9. Rome–Pisa: Fabrizio Serra Editore.

Cribiore, R. 1996. *Writing, Teachers, and Students in Graeco-Roman Egypt*. American Studies in Papyrology, 36. Atlanta: Scholars Press.

Gazda, E. K. 1978. *Guardians of the Nile: Sculptures from Karanis in the Fayoum (c. 250 BC–AD 450)*. Ann Arbor: Kelsey Museum of Archaeology.

Gazda, E. K. 2004. *Karanis: An Egyptian Town in Roman Times. Discoveries of the University of Michigan Expedition to Egypt (1924–1935)*, 2nd ed. with new introduction and bibliography by T. G. Wilfong. Ann Arbor: Kelsey Museum of Archaeology.

Haatvedt, R. A., and Peterson, E. E. 1964. *Coins from Karanis: The University of Michigan Excavations 1924–1935*. Ann Arbor: Kelsey Museum of Archaeology.

Haeckl, A. E., and Spelman, K. C. 1977. *The Gods of Egypt in the Graeco-Roman Period*. Ann Arbor: Kelsey Museum of Archaeology.

Harden, D. B. 1936. *Roman Glass from Karanis Found by the University of Michigan Archaeological Expedition in Egypt, 1924–29*. University of Michigan Studies, Humanistic Series, 41. Ann Arbor: University of Michigan Press.

Hayes, J. L. 1972. *Late Roman Pottery*. London: British School in Rome.

Hooper, F. 1961. *Funerary Stelae from Kom Abou Billou*. Kelsey Museum of Archaeology Studies, 1. Ann Arbor: Kelsey Museum of Archaeology.

Johnson, B. 1981. *Pottery from Karanis: Excavations of the University of Michigan*. Kelsey Museum of Archaeology Studies, 7. Ann Arbor: University of Michigan Press.

Kasser, R., and Satzinger, H. 1982. "L'idiome du P. Mich.5421 (trouvé à Karanis, nord-est du Fayoum)." *Wiener Zeitschrift für die Kunde des Morgenlandes* 74:15–32.

Keenan, J. G. 2003. "Deserted Villages: From the Ancient to the Medieval Fayyum." *Bulletin of the American Society of Papyrologists* 40:119–139.

Kelsey Museum 1980. *Art of the Ancient Weaver: Textiles from Egypt (4th–12th Centuries AD)*. Ann Arbor: Kelsey Museum of Archaeology.

Maguire, E. D., Maguire, H. P., and Duncan-Flowers, M. J. 1989. *Art and Holy Powers in the Early Christian House*. Illinois Byzantine Studies, 2. Urbana: University of Illinois Press.

Pollard, N. 1998. "The Chronology and Economic Condition of Late Roman Karanis: An Archaeological Reassessment." *Journal of the American Research Center in Egypt* 35:147–162.

Renner, T. 1979. "Three New Homerica on Papyrus." *Harvard Studies in Classical Philology* 83:311–337.

Rübsam, W. J. R. 1974. *Götter und Kulte im Faijum während der griechisch-römisch-byzantinischen Zeit*. Marburg Lahn: E. Symon.

Shier, L. A. 1978. *Terracotta Lamps from Karanis, Egypt: Excavations of the University of Michigan*. Kelsey Museum of Archaeology Studies, 3. Ann Arbor: University of Michigan Press.

Strong, D., and Brown, D. 1976. *Roman Crafts*. London: Duckworth.

Wilburn, A. T. 2012. *Materia Magica: The Archaeology of Magic in Roman Egypt, Cyprus, and Spain*. New Texts from Ancient Cultures. Ann Arbor: University of Michigan Press.

Wilfong, T. G. 1997. *Women and Gender in Ancient Egypt: From Prehistory to Late Antiquity*. Ann Arbor: Kelsey Museum of Archaeology.

Wilfong, T. G. 2010. "The University of Michigan Excavation of Karanis (1924–1935): Images from the Kelsey Museum Photographic Archives." In C. Riggs, ed., *The Oxford Handbook of Roman Egypt*. Oxford: Oxford University Press, 233–243.

Wilson, L. M. 1933. *Ancient Textiles from Egypt in the University of Michigan Collection*. University of Michigan Studies, Humanistic Series, 31. Ann Arbor: University of Michigan Press.

Youtie, H. C., Schuman, V. B., and Pearl, O. M. 1936–1939. *Tax Rolls from Karanis in Two Volumes (Michigan Papyri, Vol. IV, Part I–II)*. University of Michigan Studies, Humanistic Series, 42–43. Ann Arbor: University of Michigan Press.

RESEARCH

The presence of so much archival and artifactual material from the Karanis excavations at the University of Michigan has encouraged a wide range of Michigan students, staff, and faculty to do research on Karanis from a variety of approaches. A number of research projects came together in connection with the "Karanis Revealed" exhibition, while other projects not directly related to the exhibition emerged at the time of the exhibition. The articles that follow give a sampling of recent research on Karanis at the University of Michigan—from in-depth articles on artifacts and papyri, to wider examinations of archaeological context and new archaeological fieldwork, to experimental explorations of sound at Karanis. Each of these essays gives a taste of research on Karanis to come.

A Leather Cuirass Discovered at Karanis, Fayum, Egypt from the Late 3rd and Early 4th Centuries AD

Andrew W. S. Ferrara

The presence of the military and soldiers in the history of Karanis is a well-established fact. Many of the initial settlers of the site during the reign of Ptolemy II Philadelphos (282–246 BC) were most likely Macedonian soldiers, gifted grants of land for their service. During the 1st and 2nd centuries AD, many Roman soldiers settled in the village after having completed their tenure in the army, their positions and activities recorded in papyri. From the 3rd century onward, however, there is no information, textual or archaeological, pertaining to soldiers in the village, with one exception. In 1925, during the first year of excavation, the Michigan team unearthed a significant piece of leather armor from house 193, room A (KM 3631, object **138** in the catalogue of objects above). Though no detailed archaeological information was recorded, the material from elsewhere in the structure suggests that the armor be dated to between AD 250 and 350. This then represents the "only" piece of military equipment from the village beyond the 2nd century and therefore opens new avenues to understanding Karanis's position within the later imperial Roman martial structure.

The Karanis armor consists of rows of individual leather scales, sewn together in lines and then each row layered underneath the adjacent upper level. The scales are attached to each other by two leather thongs threaded through two sets of holes, lacing out and then back in the front, the pattern repeated through the back of the adjacent scale. The rows of scales are connected to each other by an additional thong threaded in the same manner, though it only enters every three to four scales. The scales, on average, have the dimensions of 5.6 cm in length, 2.1 cm in width, and 3.9 mm in thickness, while the thongs are between 1.5 and 3.5 mm in width. In addition, some parts of the armor retain a supplementary leather edging, which appears to have encompassed the outer edge of the piece. Furthermore, there appears to have been a leather backing covering the reverse side of the rows, though this material is of a different type from that used to form the scales themselves. Finally, traces of pigment have been noted on the leather, and their high iron content indicates the application of red paint/dye (see the technical discussion on pp. 129–139 below).

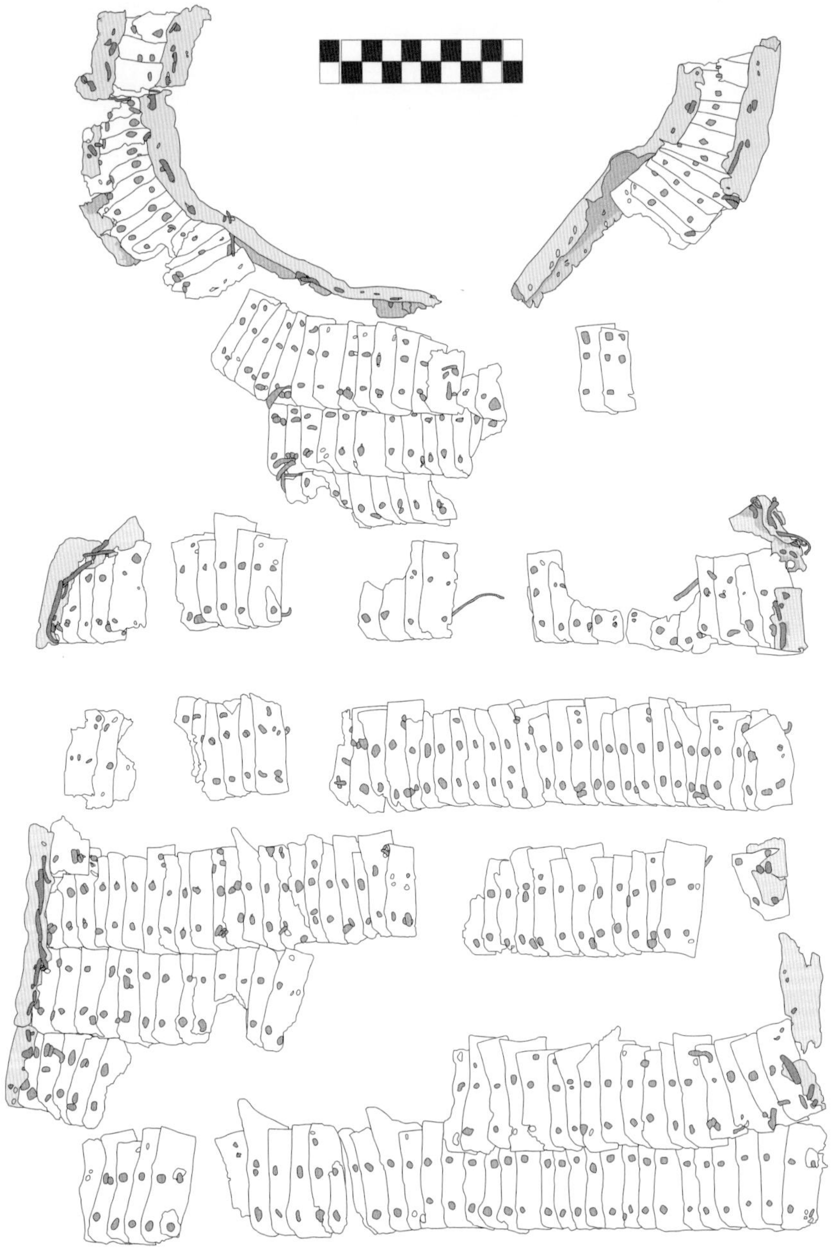

Fig. 41. Reconstruction of Karanis leather armor, **138** (KM 3631; drawing by Lorene Sterner).

Fig. 43. Curator Terry Wilfong, Curatorial Assistant Andrew Ferrara, and Conservator Claudia Chemello discuss the layout of the leather cuirass.

Fig. 42. Photograph of cuirass after treatment, as exhibited.

That the color can be noted only on portions of individual scales, and the iron peak does not occur equally across the rows, points to the fact that paint was applied after the armor's assemblage and not to the entirety of the artifact. From the proportions of the existing piece, and the various arrangements of edged rows, the armor seems most likely to have been designed as a cuirass for a torso. The reconstruction (figs. 41–43) reveals a front panel with scale row shoulder pieces, which would have continued into a back panel of leather rows, or attached to a textile rear piece. The primary restriction on further investigation of the artifact comes from its extremely brittle nature, which limits its handling and the possibility of comparison and identification.

No exact parallels to the Karanis armor appear among surviving Roman military equipment. This is due most likely to the perishable nature of leather and the inhospitable climate of most of the empire. The surviving similar pieces of chest armor are all of metal. The cuirass is constructed in a manner most similar to *lorica squamata* (scale armor) and *lorica lamellar*, though there are differences between both types and the Karanis example. With *lorica squamata*, the scales are attached to each other and to a backing fabric, and, as noted above, no backing textile has been discovered on the sample piece (Southern and Ramsey 1996, 97). Traditional *lorica lamellar*, on the other hand, has no backing material but has the plates overlapping upward, which differentiates it from the Karanis material, where the scales go downward. The closest example is actually a piece of thigh (rather than chest) armor that was excavated at Dura-Europos in modern-day Syria. This artifact has scales attached to each other and does not have a backing textile. The plates also overlap downward, covering the structural lacing behind them (James 2004, 122–124). That this comparable piece was also found in the eastern half of the empire points not only to the compatibility of the climate with preservation but also the possibility of such leather-styled armor being more extensively used across the eastern regions due to its appropriateness to the hot and dry environment.

There are, however, some deductions about the Karanis armor that may be made from the information available. The piece would have been costly to produce given the scraping and conditioning of the leather as well as the process of forming the scales and assembling the overall structure. It seems unlikely that the scales were attached directly to any textile as no fibers have been discovered upon examination. The armor would most likely have slipped over the head and either laced to the opposite backed rows or have been secured with a separate belt, like a tabard. (This is difficult to determine as none of the edge pieces have additional lacing, but little of this edging survives.) Material considerations make it unlikely that this armor would have been used in combat. Given the thickness of the scales and the minimal protection around the shoulders and neck, it seems highly unlikely that the garment would have offered much in the way of protection against swords or spears. Arrows might have been defended against more easily, though this would also have depended upon the layers of material worn underneath the scale rows. In general, however, the cuirass would have been most useful against knives, clubs, and the like, rather than any more elite weaponry. This specific orientation away from intensive combat, along with the noted unlikelihood of private commission, points to the high possibility of the armor stemming from the *limitanei* section of the Roman army.

During the period in question, the Roman Empire was in a state of flux, morphing into what would become the Byzantine state, and the military was changing along with it. Unfortunately, there is little documentation or archaeological evidence about the army from this time, and even less pertaining to Egypt specifically, so some generalizations must be made. One major shift that occurred within the military was the split between the units that made up part of the field armies (*comitatenses*) and those placed at the forts on the frontiers (*limitanei*), a gradual process that seems to have begun under Diocletian (284–305) and continued under Constantine (307–337) (Goldsworthy 2003, 202). The *limitanei* contained several different types of units, including the old auxiliary corps of infantry cohorts and cavalry *alae*. The role of the *limitanei* was primarily to patrol and garrison the frontier, as well as collecting annual state taxes, offering judicial administration, escorting dignitaries, etc. While they were able to handle simple external attacks and public disorder, anything beyond that would require the intervention of the *comitatenses* (Goldsworthy 2003, 202).

The armor would seem to correspond perfectly to the role of the *limitanei*, placing it within a military context and yet not one that would be involved in extensive warfare. The policies of the *limitanei* offer further explanations for the cuirass's discovery in Karanis. As the corps was associated with specific camps in the frontier regions, troops tended to become integrated with the area around their fortifications, owning land and raising families (Alston 1995, 151–155). Recruitment for the *limitanei* involved the obligatory enlistment of the sons of soldiers and enforced conscription from the land around the forts (MacDowall 1995, 9–10). Additionally, while the field armies were supplied with equipment from state manufacturing camps (*fabricae*), the *limitanei* produced their own weaponry, the more elaborate equipment being individually commissioned (Coulston 1990, 150). Such articles would then be personal property, and thus remain with the soldiery after retirement, which might explain the cuirass's discovery in Karanis.

With regard to the likelihood of a *limitanei* soldier in the region, two groups have been identified within the Fayum during the period of investigation. One was the Cohors (infantry) Numidarum, based at Narmouthis at the start of the 4th century, though the unit appears to have left the area by the 340s (Bell 1962, 13). The other, and considerably better documented, force was the Ala Quinta Praelectorum, a cavalry division based at the fort in Dionysias. It is, in fact, from this company that much of the information regarding the role for *limitanei* within the Roman military in general stems, due to the extensive papyri archive of Flavius Abinnaeus, commander of the *alae* from 342 or 346 to ca. 350 (Bell 1962, 6–12). Within the documents, soldiers from Dionysias are mentioned as collecting taxes from several villages in the Fayum including Karanis, and one particularly tantalizing papyrus mentions, at least, an attempted recruitment from the Michigan-excavated site itself

(*P.Abinn.* 35: Bell 1962, 87–88). While it would go too far to state that the armor came from the *alae* during the time of Abinnaeus, given the evidence, it seems very possible that a *limitanei* soldier could have been based in the Fayum and owned property or lived in Karanis between ca. 250 and ca. 350.

Though no direct textual documentation exists to confirm the presence of military personnel in Karanis during the late 3rd and early 4th centuries, the excavation of the cuirass and the potential circumstances seem to indicate that at least one soldier lived there during the period in question. If he was a member of the *limitanei* (as strongly suggested by the armor), his duties most likely revolved around establishing the manifestation of imperial authority and gathering of military taxes on the frontier. The well-made cuirass would have both offered protection against unruly civilians and acted as a badge of status, with its red dye perhaps indicating a painted insignia or symbol emblazoned on it. Whether the soldier was a native of the village or owned property there, either during service or in retirement, will remain undetermined, each option posing more questions. The evidence does, however, raise the possibility of other soldiers living in Karanis after the 2nd century, which would represent a continuation of the tradition of military personnel being based in that village, and in the Fayum region as a whole.

Bibliography

Alston, R. 1995. *Soldier and Society in Roman Egypt: A Social History*. London: Routledge.

Bell, H. I., et al. 1962. *The Abinnaeus Archive: Papers of a Roman Officer in the Reign of Constantius II*. Oxford: Clarendon Press.

Coulston, J. C. N. 1990. "Later Roman Armour, 3rd–6th Centuries AD." *Journal of Roman Military Equipment Studies* 1:139–160.

Goldsworthy, A. 2003. *The Complete Roman Army*. London: Thames & Hudson.

James, S. 2004. *The Excavations at Dura-Europos Conducted by Yale University and the French Academy of Inscriptions and Letters 1928 to 1937: Final Report VII: The Arms and Armour and Other Military Equipment*. Oxford: Oxbow Books.

MacDowall, S. 1995. *Late Roman Cavalryman AD 236–565*. Oxford: Osprey.

Southern, P., and Dixon, K. R. 1996. *The Late Roman Army*. London: B. T. Batsford.

Examination and Conservation Treatment of a Roman Leather Cuirass in the Collection of the Kelsey Museum of Archaeology

Claudia Chemello

In 2011, the Kelsey Museum of Archaeology planned a display of archaeological artifacts from the site of Karanis, Egypt, entitled "Karanis Revealed." The artifacts, excavated by the University of Michigan in the 1924–1925 Karanis field season, included fragments of Roman leather body armor, thought to be a cuirass. The misshapen, fragmentary, and extremely fragile pieces of the cuirass have been stored in various environments since excavation and were eventually accessioned into the collection of the Kelsey Museum. The process of examination and documentation of the armor is described, as well as the problems associated with a past treatment that used oil to preserve the leather, its consequences, and the conservation options for treatment.

Description of the Armor

The cuirass consists of numerous rectangular pieces of leather sewn together to form overlapping scales. The armor, although made from leather, is similar in appearance to the metal armor type *lorica squamata*, the so-called scale armor formed from rectangular metal lamellae. The armor has previously been identified in Kelsey Museum accession records as a cuirass, referring to body armor for the torso, although not enough of the cuirass survives to make an accurate assessment of its exact placement on the body.

Other examples of this type of leather armor are rare. An extensive literature search produced only one example of a similar type of leather armor, excavated at the site of Dura Europos by the Yale University/French Academy excavations in 1928–1937. Among the objects excavated at this site were three pieces of leather armor described as thigh armor (Yale numbers 1938.5999.1009 and 1938.5999.1143). These pieces are made from individual rectangular leather scales laced together with leather thong. Although made from leather, the scales differ in size and shape from those of the Karanis armor, and the lacing system is different.

The overall color of the leather cuirass from the Kelsey's collections is medium brown, with some areas quite darkened from the effects of surface dirt as well

Fig. 44. Overall view of the leather cuirass before treatment (photo author).

as darkening caused by oil staining from a previous treatment. Other areas, including most of the reverse side, are generally a light tan color. The outer surface of the leather is somewhat smooth in appearance, but the inner, or flesh, side is mostly rough, with a fibrous appearance (there are some exceptions where the inner side is smoother). This part of the skin, called the *corium*, is composed of a network of fibrous collagen bundles, clearly visible on the Karanis cuirass. The leather appears to have layers of tissue remaining on the *corium*, as if the skin were not completely scraped. On the outer surface of the leather, called the grain layer, hair follicles are clearly visible on many of the scales, and when viewed with magnification the follicle pattern resembles calf or cow skin (Kite and Thomson 2006). The follicles are numerous, close together, and somewhat regular. One or two of the scales preserve small patches of animal hair that are short and white/gray in color.

The armor survives in six large fragments that are wider than 13.5 cm, as well as nine medium-sized fragments that are wider than 5 cm, with multiple small fragments and a tray of tiny fragments. In addition to the lamellar scale armor fragments, there are multiple fragments of thin leather that appear to have detached from a lining sewn onto the inner side of the cuirass. On several of the larger fragments, the lining remains attached to the armor. In addition, there are strips of edge binding, some still in place on the armor and some detached.

Several of the scales show areas of red color on the outer surface, possibly red pigment. The color was applied after the armor was constructed, as indicated by the fact that usually one half of the scale is missing the red color where it was originally shielded by the neighboring, overlapping scale.

Construction Overview

As described, the armor consists of four main elements: the small, thick scales or lamellae; the thin leather lining; the edge binding; and the leather thong that stitches all the elements together (fig. 44).

Scales: The lamellar scales are generally rectangular in shape and appear to be cut on all sides. A few have ends that are clipped on a diagonal. The average length of each scale is 5.6 cm, with variations as small as 4.9 cm and as large as 6.2 cm. The average width of each scale is 2.1 cm, with variations as small as 1.7 cm and as large as 2.9 cm. The average thickness of the scales is 3.9 mm, with a variation from 1.5 mm to 4.0 mm. The averages were taken from a random sample of 12 scales.

Each horizontal row of scales is arranged in an overlapping pattern. Each scale overlaps its neighbor so that it covers the right, vertical edge. The rows are then stacked and lapped, overlapping from the top down. Three rows of stitching hold the scales together. Two rows of stitching pass through each scale, stitched through two holes at each point, holding each scale to the next. These rows of running stitches pass once through each scale at the bottom and once about two-thirds of the way up. The third row of stitching holds the rows of scales together vertically and is stitched through two holes. These stitches are much longer and straddle several scales; on average about every third scale is caught by a stitch. The holes for stitching were made through the leather from the front to the back, with the occasional hole made from back to front. The instrument used to make the hole appears to have been roughly oval shaped.

Fig. 45. Detail of the exterior surface of cuirass fragment, with overlapping scales and stitching visible (photo author).

The largest of the fragments preserves four partial rows of scales, with fragmentary edge binding and lining *in situ*. Other smaller chunks preserve two and single rows of scales, some with edge binding *in situ*. One fragment of three rows of scales is curved along the top row.

Stitching: The leather thong used for stitching the scales together is approximately 1.5 to 3.5 mm in width, with a roughly rectangular cross section (fig. 45). The thong is mostly light tan to beige in color, is twisted in places, and often narrows toward one end, possibly to assist with threading it through the hole.

Lining: Thin, light tan to medium brown colored leather was used as a lining on the interior side of the armor, covering the stitching and scales. The lining survives in multiple, small, detached fragments and remains *in situ* on at least five fragments. The lining is stitched in place on the edges underneath the edge binding.

Edge binding: The edge binding is a thin strip of dark brown colored leather, approximately 4 cm wide, which wraps around the edge of the armor from front to back and is sewn in place with leather thong through the scales and lining. Edge binding is preserved *in situ* on ten fragments, and there are numerous detached fragments of the binding.

Treatment and Storage History

Prior to acquisition into the collection of the Kelsey Museum, documentation of previous treatment(s) of the leather cuirass is unknown. Several fragments of the cuirass were exhibited in 1983 in an exhibition at the Kelsey Museum entitled "Karanis: An Egyptian Town in Roman Times." In 1982, during preparation for the exhibition, the cuirass was examined and treated by the museum's conservator at that time, Amy Rosenberg. During examination, Rosenberg noted that the cuirass had undergone previous treatment. Rosenberg describes the leather in her 1982 report as "exuding oily spots onto paper." A wide variety of dressings for leather are known, especially those that involve fats or oils to increase flexibility and waterproofing properties. Archaeological conservation was a relatively new field of study in 1924–1925, the years of the first field seasons at Karanis, when the leather was excavated. One prominent scientist who stood out at that time for his early impact on the field of archaeological conservation was Alfred Lucas (Gilberg 1997). Lucas authored a seminal work entitled *Antiques, Their Restoration and Preservation* (Lucas 1924). In this work, Lucas describes several treatments for preserving dried archaeological leather, including the use of castor oil, lanoline, sperm oil, and vaseline. Techniques for treatment of dried archaeological leather that became common in the 1960s and '70s include impregnation of the leather with polyethylene glycol and vaseline, at high temperature (Plenderleith and Werner 1971).

Following examination, Rosenberg undertook treatment of the leather, presumably to remove some of the oil. Her treatment records that several solvents, as well as polyethylene glycol, were tested for surface cleaning, without success. Treatment then proceeded to soaking of the fragments in acetone, presumably to remove the oil, a procedure that "removed a yellow stain" (Rosenberg 1982).

Little is known of the storage environment or transport conditions of the leather following excavation, during transfer from Egypt to Ann Arbor, or when it first arrived in Ann Arbor. The majority of the museum's collections were stored on the second floor of the 1890s Newberry Hall building prior to 1994. Between 1993 and 1994, the museum remodeled the third floor of the building, adding more floor space to house the Sensitive Artifact Facility and Environment (SAFE), a space with improved climate control. Since 2009, the leather has been stored in a new climate-controlled storage space in the Upjohn Exhibit Wing, the museum's new addition.

Condition of the Leather

Survival of the leather is almost certainly due to the arid conditions in Egypt at the site of Karanis, which favored the preservation of organic materials including basketry, wood, textile, and items of food such as seeds and grains. The condition of the leather upon excavation is unknown, although presumably the high temperatures on site and desiccated conditions had already led to some degree of permanent damage due to loss of water present in the leather. Damage may have included loss of flexibility, shrinkage, tearing, and cracking. Fluctuations in relative humidity (RH), particularly low RH, highly possible during years of storage in uncontrolled environments, may have led to further deterioration of the already-desiccated leather.

The pre-1982 treatment of the leather with oil has further contributed to its darkened and brittle state. All of the leather scales appear to have received the oil treatment, but the edge binding and the leather lining show no evidence of the oil. In some of the break areas, the entire thickness of the leather appears to be impregnated with oil. In these areas, the fibrous structure of the leather is no longer visible, and, when viewed under magnification, the cross section reveals a shiny, orange-brown dried residue through the entire thickness of the scale, with no collagen fibers visible. The surface of many of the scales has a shiny appearance, with some areas orange-brown in color. The treatment in 1982 to remove the oil by immersing the entire cuirass in acetone almost certainly removed any moisture that remained in the leather, causing further irreversible stiffness.

The majority of the fragments are buckled and deformed, and many are delaminating. Overall, the leather is extremely fragile and fragmentary, to the extent that handling of the pieces during examination and treatment was kept to an absolute minimum to avoid further breakage and loss. Numerous pieces are cracked and broken, with a lot of small, disassociated loose fragments. In addition to the darkening and embrittlement, some pieces of the leather, notably the dark colored edge binding, appear somewhat powdery.

All the fragments are dirty; the dirt varies from a thick, muddy accretion, with embedded grass, to a thinner dusty coating. Insect damage is visible on many pieces, with damage varying from loss of the grain surface only to areas eaten all the way through. The lining is the thinnest piece of leather and as such was the most readily subject to damage. Most of the lining has been lost, with some small sections still stitched in place on the inner side of the armor and the remainder as tiny, loose fragments (fig. 46).

Assessment and Treatment

In consultation with curatorial staff, conservators decided that the overall approach to treatment would be preventive in nature and follow principles of minimal intervention. The condition of the leather and its long-term stability were critical

Fig. 46. Detail of various fragments, showing staining and darkening due to previous oil treatment, deformation, and surface dirt (photo author).

considerations, as was the level of deterioration already sustained by previous treatments. An added and significant obstacle was the extreme embrittlement of the leather, causing difficulties in handling. It was further considered to be too aggressive to introduce yet another material, possibly in the form of a consolidant in an attempt to make the leather more pliable, with an unsure outcome and possible irreversibility. Based on the results of humidification tests on samples of the leather with water and solvent vapors, this proved to be a wise course of action.

The first major priority for the leather was full documentation. The pieces were photographed digitally and a condition report recorded into the museum's conservation database. All of the pieces of the armor were described, including the construction and sewing technique, measurements of the individual components, and description of their state of preservation. Arrangement of the fragments during examination afforded a greater insight into their possible layout and position on the torso, and close examination clarified details that were previously unknown or unrecorded. These included the fact that the garment was originally lined, the correct orientation of the scales, the survival of areas of red color on the outer surface, and the likely sequence of construction.

Following documentation, all pieces of the leather were gently cleaned using a soft brush and low suction vacuum cleaner under magnification. Further cleaning was achieved with soft synthetic cosmetic sponges to dislodge areas of resistant dirt. Barely moistened cotton wool swabs of 50:50 deionized water and ethanol were gently rolled over the surface in discrete areas to further remove dirt and grime. Care was taken not to overdampen the surface, to reduce the possibility that it would become tacky and shiny from reaction with the oil, and to avoid the possibility of localized swelling or staining.

Reshaping of the leather was discussed as a possibility for some parts of the cuirass that were deformed, particularly pieces that appeared to belong to the shoulder and upper torso area. This option was ultimately rejected for several reasons, the most significant of which was the fact that, when tested, the leather scales (the most brittle component of the cuirass) were not rehydrated or softened by either water or solvent vapor and were made slightly tacky by solvent vapors. The edge binding and lining were slightly softened by the water and solvent vapor, but they were also significantly darkened by both. In light of the difficulty of introducing moisture into the leather, the introduction of a consolidant to allow for reshaping was not considered feasible due to the effect of the previous treatment with oil. In addition, the leather can withstand very little pressure without breaking. Reshaping was also not practical without firm stylistic information about the position of the individual pieces of armor on the body.

Tanning Identification

The leather was spot tested for the presence of vegetable tannins with a simple, nondestructive test to establish the presence or absence of vegetable tannins using iron(III) sulfate. The iron(III) ferric ions react with the phenolic compounds present in vegetable-tanned leathers, producing a dark blue or green coloration (Odegaard 2000). Vegetable tanning was the most common form of tanning in use during the Roman period (Cronyn 1990; van Driel-Murray 2002).

The test was performed on tiny fibers of the leather removed from the reverse side. The solution was also applied directly to an unobtrusive area on the front surface of the leather, on pieces of scale, the stitching, the lining, and the edge binding. In each case the sample was viewed under magnification, and no color change was observed. While the result may initially indicate that the leather is not vegetable tanned, modification of the leather during burial, for example by chemical decay, and post-excavation treatment with an unidentified oil may have affected the result and need to be investigated further. The result may also indicate that the leather was not tanned or tanned using another method.

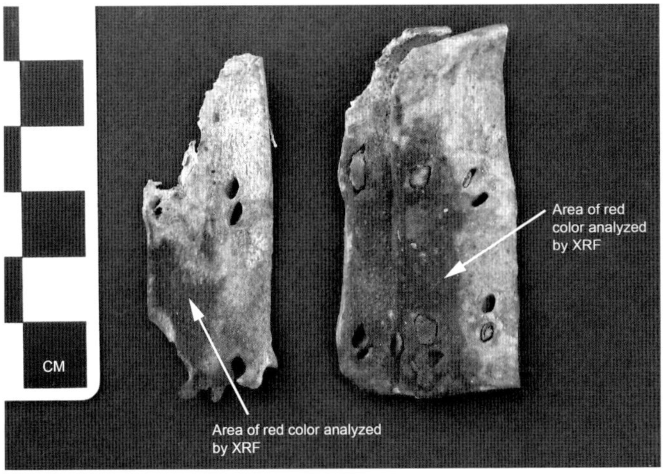

Fig. 47. Detail of the two scales with strong red coloration visible on the outer surface (photo author).

Investigation of the Red Color

As described, several of the scales from the leather cuirass appear to have areas of red pigmentation on the front surface. The application of color appears to be deliberate and was made after the scales were sewn together, as the color is not present where a scale was overlapped by an adjacent scale. Examination with optical microscopy revealed that in some areas the color was powdery and matte in appearance. In other areas it was somewhat hidden underneath the darkened coating of oil.

X-ray fluorescence spectroscopy (XRF) was used to identify major elements in areas of particularly strong red coloration on two detached scales (fig. 47). The red areas were analyzed directly with a handheld Brucker Tracer III-SD instrument. The XRF analysis produced a spectrum consisting of a series of peaks. The energy at which each peak occurs and its height correspond to the element present and its quantity. XRF measurements recorded very strong amounts of iron, as well as small amounts of calcium, probably from the burial environment. The large amount of iron detected in the red areas suggests that these areas were colored with an iron compound. Whether the iron originated from a mineral or organic source and whether it was applied as a pigment or as a dye require further investigation.

Future Research

The display of the Roman leather cuirass in the collection of the Kelsey Museum presented an important opportunity to learn about the condition and preservation of this unique artifact. Although the fragments of the cuirass are extremely deteriorated, with a largely unknown treatment and storage history, the survival of this artifact is quite remarkable. The extreme fragility of the material has guided conservation efforts, with the principle of minimal intervention being the fundamental concern of current conservation efforts.

The results of this initial investigation have opened numerous avenues for future research. Discovering what kind of oil was used to coat the leather would be helpful in determining whether its harmful effects on the leather can be lessened. The effect of the oil on the skin may have compromised further technical examination, but the use of the oil itself provides valuable information about historical conservation treatments and their effects over time.

Additional investigation of the skin might provide further clues as to the curing and/or tanning technique used for the skin. The study of DNA extracted from the leather could firmly determine the animal species used in the manufacture of the armor and confirm visual observations, although the extraction of DNA from archaeological specimens is extremely difficult since often no DNA survives in ancient tissues and what little does survive is frequently contaminated (Hofreiter 2001). Further study of the red coloration could help determine the source of the color and how and why it was applied, providing clues to the decoration of military armor.

Acknowledgments

The author would like to thank Terry Wilfong for including this incredible and unique object in the exhibition "Karanis Revealed," providing an opportunity for examination and treatment. The examination and conservation work would not have been possible without the help of my colleague Suzanne Davis, who helped examine, describe, and document the cuirass. Andrew Ferrara gave many helpful insights into the history, use, and possible configuration of the armor. Caroline Roberts, then Samuel H. Kress Conservation Fellow at the Kelsey Museum, shared helpful information and references about the conservation of leather, and Bruce Kaiser of Bruker Elemental generously agreed to loan a portable XRF to the Kelsey Museum for several weeks for analytical work. Lorene Sterner provided assistance with the digital images.

Bibliography

Cronyn, J. M. 1990. *The Elements of Archaeological Conservation*. London: Routledge.

Driel-Murray, C. van 2002. "Practical Consideration of a Field Test for the Identification of Ancient Vegetable Tanned Leather." *Journal of Archaeological Science* 29:17–21.

Falcão, L., and Araújo, E. M. M. 2011. "Tannins Characterisation in New and Historic Vegetable Tanned Leather Fibres by Spot Tests." *Journal of Cultural Heritage* 12:149–156.

Ganiaris, H., Keene, S., and Starling, K. 1982. "A Comparison of Some Treatments for Excavated Leather." *The Conservator* 6:12–24.

Gilberg, M. 1997. "Alfred Lucas: Egypt's Sherlock Holmes." *Journal of the American Institute for Conservation* 36:31–48.

Goubitz, O. 1984. "The Drawing and Registration of Archaeological Footwear." *Studies in Conservation* 29:187–196.

Groennman-van Watteringe, W., Killan, M., and Londen, H. van 1999. 'The Curing of Hides and Skins in European Prehistory." *Antiquity* 73:884–890.

Handt, O., Höss, M., et al. 1994. "Ancient DNA: Methodological Challenges." *Experientia* 50:525–529.

Hofreiter, M., et al. 2001. "Ancient DNA." *Nature* 2:353–359.

James, S. 2004. *The Excavations at Dura-Europos Conducted by Yale University and the French Academy of Inscriptions and Letters 1928 to 1937: Final Report VII: The Arms and Armour and Other Military Equipment*. Oxford: Oxbow Books.

Kite, M., and Thomson, R. 2006. *Conservation of Leather*. London: Butterworth-Heinemann.

Lucas, A. 1924. *Antiques, Their Restoration and Preservation*. London: Edward Arnold.

Odegaard, N., Carroll, S., and Zimmt, W. S. 2000. *Material Characterization Tests for Objects of Art and Archaeology*. London: Archetype Publications.

Plenderleith, H. J., and Werner, A. E. E. 1971. *The Conservation of Antiquities and Works of Art*. London: Oxford University Press.

Rosenberg, A. 1982. Conservation Record, Kelsey Museum Conservation Laboratory, 31 August 1982.

Sully, D. M. 1992. "Humidification: The Reshaping of Leather, Skin and Gut Objects for Display, The Conservation of Leathercraft and Leather Objects." In P. Hallebeek, M. Kite, and C. Calnan, eds., *ICOM Symposium*. London: ICOM, 50–53.

Wills, B. 2000. "A Review of the Conservation Treatment of a Roman-Egyptian Cuirass and Helmet Made from Crocodile Skin." *The Conservator* 24:80–88.

Wills, B. 2001. *Leather Wet and Dry: Current Treatments in the Conservation of Waterlogged and Desiccated Archaeological Leather*. London: Archetype Publications.

A Skeleton from the Michigan Karanis Excavation

Thomas Landvatter

The University of Michigan excavated four burials during the first season of work at Karanis in 1924. These presumably are from Karanis's cemetery, which has still not been properly excavated. However, there are no records indicating the location of these burials or the purpose behind their excavation. The only available records are a series of photographs showing each burial *in situ*, division photographs showing the extant remains of each burial disarticulated and grouped according to bone type, and tags associated with each skeleton commenting on the sex and basic pathology of the individual—some of which information has proved to be incorrect. All four burials were lost for some time, until 2006, when they were found in the University of Michigan Museum of Anthropology and returned to the Kelsey Museum to be with the rest of the Karanis finds.

Burial 1924.100 (**140** in the catalogue above) is the skeleton of an adult female, aged between 55 and 60 years. Photographs (fig. 40 above) show that she had a simple burial (inhumation), with no grave goods as far as is known, and that she was not mummified. Her arms were placed at her side, her hands over her pelvis. At some point between her arrival in Ann Arbor in the 1920s and her transfers to and from the Anthropology Museum, several bones seem to have gone missing or became mixed with the other burials; the division photograph (fig. 48) shows examples of bone that are not present in the individual as she exists in the Kelsey today. The initial study of bone pathology, conducted soon after arrival in Ann Arbor, was never published, existing solely on the aforementioned tags. Her joints show signs of relatively advanced arthritis: there is marked lipping on the knee joint of the right tibia, and the distal (wrist) joint of the right ulna shows extensive burnishing, lipping, and erosion of the joint surfaces. Her lumbar (lower) vertebrae show abnormal osteophytic lipping and porosity, conditions that weakened her spine and reduced her flexibility and capacity for movement. Such advanced arthritis is normally a sign not only of advanced age but also of hard physical labor. The most striking pathology is a fracture in the left femur (thigh bone). The neck of her femur, just below the joint with her hip, fractured completely. She lived for some time after this fracture: at her death, it was completely healed, but leaving her left leg shorter and deformed,

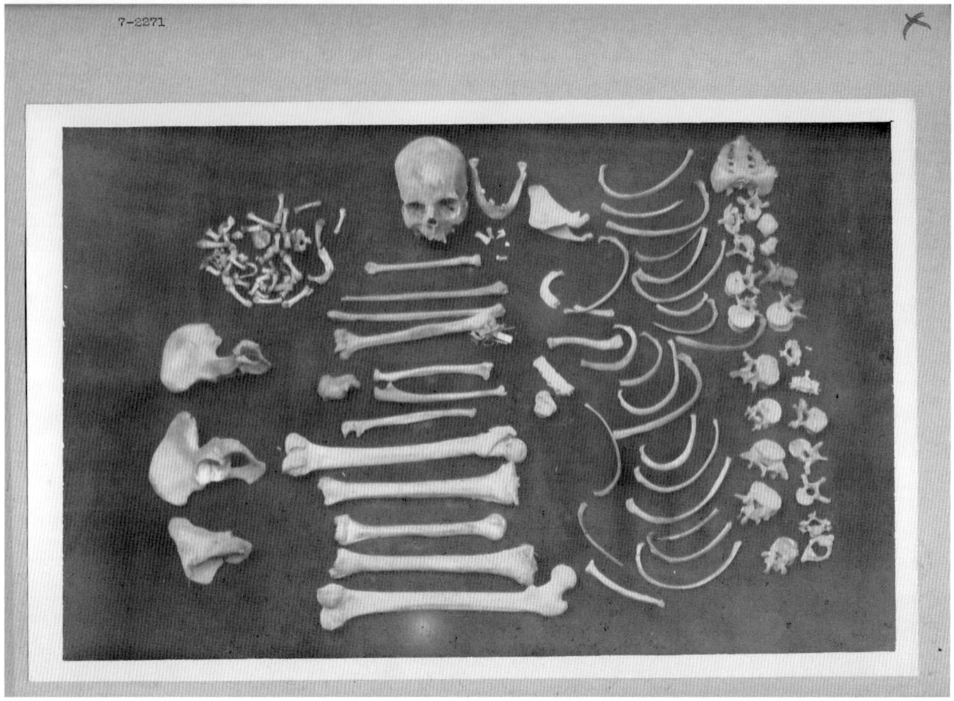

Fig. 48. Burial 1924.100, division album photograph (Kelsey Museum neg. no. 7.2271).

as well as riddled with osteoporosis due to disuse atrophy. This injury would have caused her a permanent disability for the rest of her life.

All four of these burials appear to have been extremely sparse, with no grave goods or elaborate body treatment to speak of. It is likely for this reason that the Karanis excavators ceased their work in the cemetery: it simply did not yield objects deemed to be of any value. The later excavation at Terenouthis in 1935 would provide the much-desired funerary material for the Kelsey Museum. But the burials of these individuals are intriguing precisely because of their sparseness: it is useful to be reminded that the majority of individuals at Karanis were quite poor and led hard lives. Most Egyptians—of all periods, not just the Roman—were buried in simple graves with no special treatment of any kind. The skeletons themselves, however, can shed light on these individuals' harsh existence: broken bones, arthritis, and osteoporosis. Yet this woman lived a long life despite her injuries. It is hoped that further work on these burials, as well as future work on the Karanis cemetery, will continue to shed light on the inhabitants of Karanis.

The Granary C123 Sealings from Karanis

Jennifer Gates-Foster

In 1930, excavators from the University of Michigan began work in Karanis on a mud-brick complex that would come to be known as building C123. During their room-by-room excavation, almost 300 small Nile clay sealings, or *bullae*, were discovered in the southern half of the building in the remains of the cellars and bins.[1] These tiny objects—the largest of which was a mere 9 cm—bear the impressions of seal stones on their obverse and of the objects to which they were affixed on their reverse. To their credit, the excavators took care to note their provenance and to carefully preserve the fragile clay sealings, which are now divided between the Kelsey Museum and the Egyptian Museum in Cairo.[2] Despite their diminutive size, these artifacts are an important source of information on the economic function of building C123, as well as for the visual milieu of Roman Egypt. This short article will offer an overview of this cache of sealings, outlining the scope of important issues they present for analysis and giving preliminary results of an ongoing investigation.

Building C123 was one of ten large granary buildings in the so-called C level at Karanis, which is loosely dated to the 2nd and early 3rd centuries AD (site views figs. 2 and 28, plan fig. 49). It accommodated two different types of grain storage facilities: a series of shallow bins, some with low vaulted roofs and others apparently unroofed. Bins of this type were confined to the northern courtyard of the building. Larger storage vaults in the west and south were aligned along central passageways. The southern group was arranged along either side of an east-west hall with an arched ceiling, CE in the plan. Another group of identical vaults were aligned along passageway CP running north-south. The floor of each vault was 1.5 m below the

[1] The total number of sealings in the Kelsey Museum collection from Karanis is 317, with 287 belonging to the group recovered from C123. Others were almost certainly recovered but never recorded.

[2] The Egyptian Museum houses 33 sealings from Karanis. These examples were studied by Dr. Paola Davoli, and I am grateful for her generous provision of images and descriptions for these items. Some examples from this group are discussed in Davoli 2005. The Kelsey holds 316 mud sealings from Karanis, 286 of which are from granary C123.

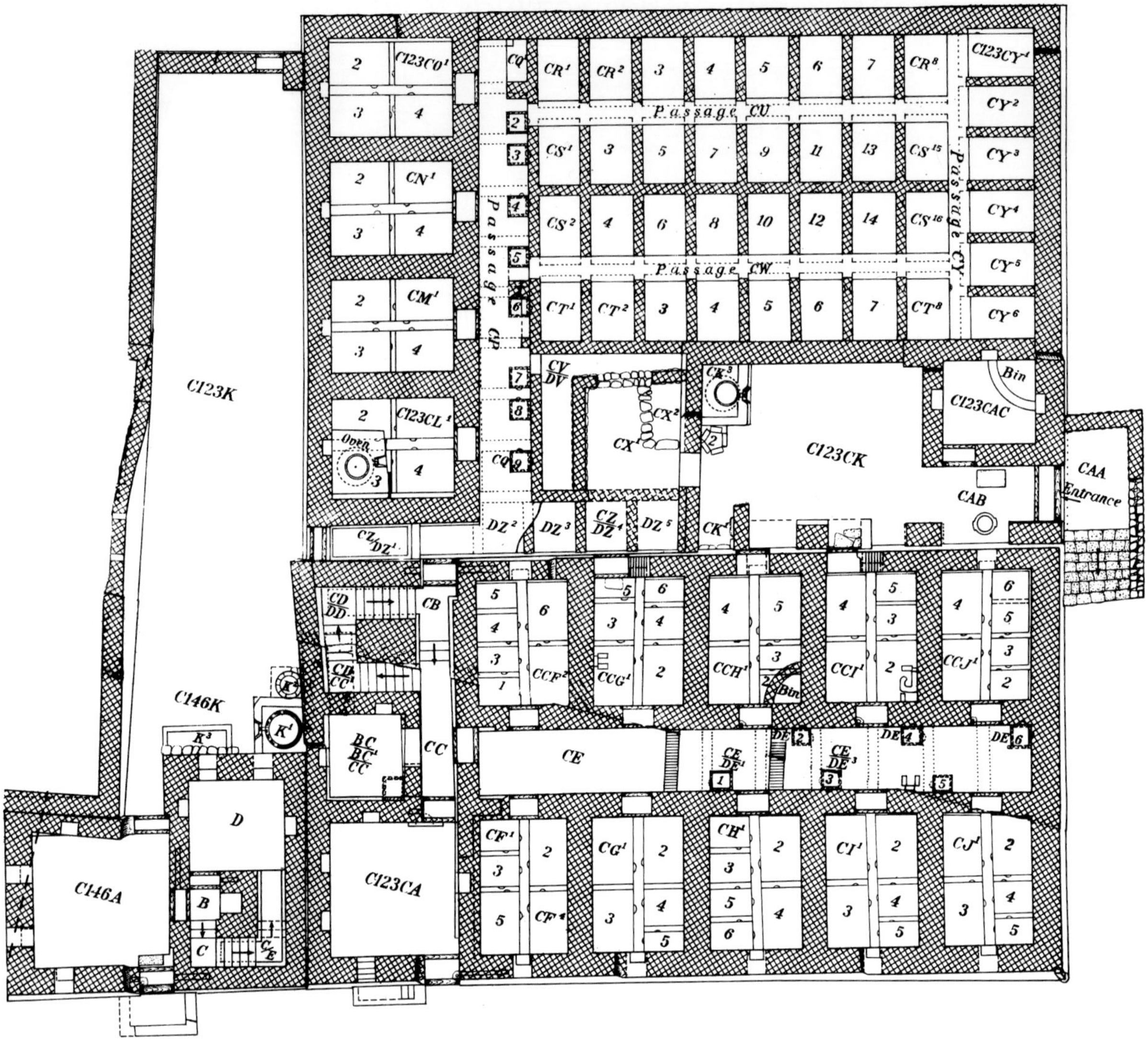

Fig. 49. Plan of granary C123 (Kelsey Museum neg. no. M8.0694).

level of the exterior passageway, and these sunken areas were cut in half by a major wall, which also functioned as a footpath to allow an individual to walk out into the room. The area on either side of this main partition was further subdivided by smaller walls, which cut the area into several small sunken compartments. These dividing walls were also provided with footholds to allow for easy access to the material in the bins.

In addition, the passageways CE and CP leading to these vaults were provided with a series of trapdoors opening into yet another smaller group of vaulted chambers. This floor plan with passageways and storage vaults was mirrored in a second floor, which was largely destroyed in antiquity. Over time, the floor level in these vaults rose, and eventually rooms CCG, CCH, and CCI were deliberately filled and converted to living quarters. Wall paintings were added to these vaults and additional doors cut into their northern wall to allow access to the northern granary bins.

The excavators recorded eleven separate and distinct findspots for the sealings, located in eight different rooms, as shown below:

Findspot 1:	room CG, bin 4
Findspot 2:	room CH, no bin specified
Findspot 3:	room CQ, bin 9
Findspot 4:	room DE, bin 1
Findspot 5:	room CCG, bin 1
Findspot 6:	room CCH, bin 1
Findspot 7:	room CCI, no bin specified
Findspot 8:	room CCI, bin 2
Findspot 9:	room CJ, fill level no bin specified
Findspot 10:	room CJ, bin 2
Findspot 11:	room CJ, bin 5

In general, these findspots are concentrated in the southern half of the structure, with CQ being the only exception. They are all found in a storage vault or in a vault beneath the floor of a passageway linking the vaults. No sealings were found in any other part of the building, most notably, none from the four vaults along passage CP.

There are 286 separate sealings from C123 in the Kelsey collection (see fig. 50 and objects **67–69** above for examples). On these objects, 45 different seals are represented. Of these 45, 19 occur on only one sealing. All but five of the sealings are impressed with a single seal, although often a sealing will carry multiple impressions of the same seal. The sealings carry images of Sarapis, Isis, Athena, Harpocrates, various animal forms, and compositions that combine Sarapis or Harpocrates with indigenous animals (Gates 2003–2004; Gates-Foster forthcoming). Greek and Egyptian deities are represented, as are Greek inscriptions and geometric devices. It is not clear how these seals were deployed, although they likely represent an individual, family, or merchant group (Vandorpe 1993; Vandorpe 2005; Wilfong 2003). Many carry magical imagery or inscriptions, making it clear that they were connected to the apotropaic and protective functions thought to be possessed by gems and amulets. The various findspots show statistically significant clusters of certain seals, suggesting that the same seal-holder—whether an individual or a group—made repeated deposits in the same location over time (fig. 50).

During the 2nd and 3rd centuries AD, Karanis was home to some ten large and seven small granaries, making it a central collection point for tax and private grain from the surrounding agricultural lands (Rickman 1980; Husselman 1952; Milne 1906). Papyrological evidence suggests that vaults and bins like those found in C123 might be rented out by individuals and groups for grain deposit and storage (Rickman 1971). Thus, the sealings might have come from containers used for the transport of grain or to mark vessels or bins with material arriving from other locations or farms. The sealings not only marked ownership but were designed to protect the contents from tampering and to ensure that a container or bin remained closed until formally opened as part of a transaction (Haighton 2010). The imagery carried by these sealings would have been an integral part of identifying and securing the contents deposited in the granary, making these images much more than decorative. As in other ancient archives, seal impressions functioned as a visual signature, and the iconography and style of these images offer rich insight into the preferences and values of those who deployed them (Henig 1997).

In addition to their obverse seal impressions, each of the 286 sealings also bears a reverse impression that is a negative of the object to which this clay was affixed while still damp. The range of reverse impression types is varied, but they can reasonably be divided into five types, with some variation among them. Type A sealings are generally flat, with only minimal curvature at the edges of the sealing. These appear to have been attached to wood, plaster, or ceramic surfaces. Type

Fig. 50. Obverse impressions of KM 24505 (left) and 24440 (right).

Fig. 51. Type B reverse impression (KM 24503).

B sealings generally form an angle, ranging from a perfect 90-degree corner (fig. 51) to a more obtuse curve that resembles the curve of a small jar. They are often marked with a strange groove that terminates in a knob of clay that remains raised, as if they were never applied to a surface. These are particularly difficult to interpret but were likely applied to the edge of a box or some other wooden container. Type C is perfectly concave and smooth on two surfaces, as if it had been wedged between two jars. Type D is rough and uneven, with impressions of vegetation and possibly basketry. Type E has no real reverse surface but was wrapped around string or cloth. All of these types usually carry the impression of string, sometimes underneath the sealing but occasionally wrapped around the exterior of the sealing and cutting into a seal impression.

The excavators postulated that these sealings all represented some kind of door sealing mechanism and might have been a way to control access to the individual vaults in this part of the granary. Although this was certainly part of how these sealings were used, the wide range of reverse impression types suggests considerably more diversity in the kinds of containers and objects to which they were applied.[3] The Kelsey sealings were likely affixed to wooden doors and boxes, ceramic jars, and to string and rope attached to these objects and to other kinds of containers (such as cloth sacks) that do not survive in the archaeological record.

Further work on the Karanis sealings corpus will focus on the iconographic choices made by the residents of the Roman Fayum, especially the range of

[3] Published examples from Bacchias, another Roman site in the Fayum, support this (Davoli 2005).

religious images that were preferred, not only at Karanis but in other villages, as symbols of identity and authenticity. In addition, full publication will include an analysis of the distribution of types in the findspots throughout the building, and the site at large, and the patterns that can be gleaned from a close study of where and how individual seals were used and to what they were affixed.

Bibliography

Davoli, P., ed. 2005. *Oggetti in argilla dall'area templare di Bakchias (El-Fayyum, Egitto). Catalogo dei rinvenimenti delle campagne di scavo 1996–2002, con una appendice di Katelijn Vandorpe.* Biblioteca degli "Studi di Egittologia e di Papirologia," 3. Pisa: Giardini Editori e Stampatori in Pisa.

Gates, J. 2003–2004. "A Clay Sealing from Karanis in the Kelsey Museum." *The University of Michigan Museums Bulletin* 15:92–95.

Gates-Foster, J. Forthcoming. *A Catalogue of the Karanis Sealing in the Kelsey Museum of Archaeology.*

Haighton, A. 2010. "Roman Methods of Authentication in the First Two Centuries AD." *Journal of the Society of Archivists* 31:29–49.

Henig, M. 1997. "Roman Sealstones." In D. Collon, ed., *7000 Years of Seals.* London: British Museum Press, 88–106.

Husselman, E. M. 1952. "The Granaries of Karanis." *Transactions and Proceedings of the American Philological Association* 83:56–73.

Milne, J. G. 1906. "Clay-Sealings from the Fayum." *The Journal of Hellenic Studies* 26:32–45.

Rickman, G. 1980. *The Corn Supply of Ancient Rome.* Oxford: Clarendon Press.

Rickman, G. 1971. *Roman Granaries and Store Buildings.* Cambridge: Cambridge University Press.

Vandorpe, K. 1993. "Seals in and on the Papyri of Greco-Roman and Byzantine Egypt." In M.-F. Boussac and A. Invernizzi, eds., *Archives and Sceaux du Monde Hellénistique: Archivi e Sigilli nel Mondo Ellenistico.* Athens: École Française d'Athènes, 231–261.

Vandorpe, K. 2005. "Sealing Containers in Greco-Roman Egypt. The Inscriptional and Papyrological Evidence." In P. Davoli, ed., *Oggetti in argilla dall'area templare di Bakchias (El-Fayyum, Egitto). Catalogo dei rinvenimenti delle campagne di scavo 1996–2002, con una appendice di Katelijn Vandorpe.* Biblioteca degli "Studi di Egittologia e di Papirologia," 3. Pisa: Giardini Editori e Stampatori in Pisa, 163–175.

Wilfong, T. 2003. "Stamp Seals and Seal Impressions from the Post-Pharaonic Period." In E. Teeter, ed., *Scarabs, Scaraboids, Seals and Seal Impressions from Medinet Habu.* Chicago: Oriental Institute Publications, 188–212.

A Rediscovered Agricultural Hinterland of Karanis

R. James Cook

The first Greek papyrus from Egypt was published in 1788. Called the *Charta Borgiana* after its owner, Cardinal Stefano Borgia, the document was a report of local labor directed toward the maintenance of one part of the Fayum irrigation system in the late 2nd century AD. Since the time of that publication, papyrologists and historians have published hundreds of additional documents that attest to the social and economic importance of irrigation in the Fayum and the staggering physical and administrative effort required to develop and maintain the canals that provided water for drinking and farming in that arid region.

Even before the excavations undertaken by the University of Michigan at the site between 1924 and 1935, scholars had begun to speculate on the possible relationships between the evolution of the irrigation system and the foundation and abandonment of Karanis and other well-preserved sites on the periphery of the Fayum. Their conclusions were, however, based entirely upon the Greek documentary evidence provided by the papyri.

Two British researchers—Gertrude Caton-Thompson, a prehistorian, and Elinor Gardner, a geologist—were the first to apply an archaeological approach when they discovered part of the ancient canal network to the north of Karanis in 1927–1928. That winter, a rare rainstorm caused parallel lines of plants to sprout in the desert. Although their research interests lay elsewhere, they realized that the seedlings indicated the presence of buried Graeco-Roman canals and recognized that the opportunity to study them would quickly evaporate. In a remarkable display of broadmindedness and dedication to scholarship, Caton-Thompson and Gardner recorded and excavated extensive segments of the canal system and several small related sites, which they published in the *The Desert Fayum* (1934).

The pioneering work of Caton-Thompson and Gardner has been largely neglected since its original publication, and few archaeological studies of canals have been conducted in Egypt in the intervening years. This omission is remarkable given both the fundamental importance of water and irrigation to life in ancient Egypt and the innovative methodologies that have been applied to the study of ancient canals in other parts of the world. While the work of Caton-Thompson

Fig. 52. Pan-Sharpened Near-Infrared Quickbird Image of Caton-Thompson and Gardner's "Canal E." The differential plant growth along the buried channel (indicated by black arrows) can be easily discerned running southeast-northwest through a series of fields and a large empty lot beside the village of Qarya Ula (data from Digital Globe 2007).

and Gardner foreshadowed numerous methodologies now used to study irrigation systems, many other developments have taken place since the 1920s. The complex range of geoarchaeological approaches that have been developed by archaeologists working in other countries form a "World Archaeology of Irrigation" that may be adapted and applied to permit interpretation at multiple scales beyond what was possible for Caton-Thompson and Gardner.

Fieldwork conducted in the Fayum by the author is a first step toward the application of these approaches to the irrigation system. During two seasons (September–December 2007 and September–December 2008), the ancient hydraulic system preserved to the north of Karanis was reexamined under the aegis of the UCLA/RUG Fayum Project. The fieldwork had two primary objectives: (1) to relocate and reassess the relict canal alignments identified by Caton-Thompson and Gardner in 1927–1928 in the light of recent methodology, and (2) to attempt to locate and assess new alignments unknown to Caton-Thompson and Gardner, particularly in proximity to Karanis.

Given the vast area under investigation, the author utilized a combination of field walking, communication with local informants, and consultation of satellite imagery in order to locate the canals. Satellite imagery was particularly useful in relocating the previously known hydraulic features amid the extensive damage to the landscape caused by modern agricultural, industrial, and military development (fig. 52). Once identified, individual channels were excavated to obtain datable evidence

Fig. 53. A narrow canal cut into the bedrock in the desert northwest of Karanis, after excavation. A smaller channel, which is visible diverging from the main channel at left, fed agricultural fields in the vicinity (photo author).

and to examine the water-borne sediments preserved in the channels. The size and shape of the sediments provide evidence for reconstructing the velocity and depth of flow in the canals and enable calculation of the total area irrigated in antiquity.

Reexamination of the landscape to the north and west of Karanis in 2007–2008 relocated many of the remaining components of the irrigation system. Excavation of sections across the alignments detected numerous subtle variations in the channels indicative of their construction techniques, phasing, and use (fig. 53). Preliminary analysis of the finds has extended the occupation history of this small part of the Fayum irrigation system from the early Ptolemaic period to the late 1st century BC or early 1st century AD. The longer period of occupation and significant number of small rural sites in the area prove that the system was not a brief, failed attempt at reclamation of the desert wasteland but a viable long-term endeavor that produced a dynamic and populated landscape.

In addition, a previously unidentified series of superimposed relict canal channels was discovered immediately to the south of Karanis. These channels and their associated berms attest to the frequent refurbishment of the system over time. Further investigation of the artifacts promises to provide more detailed dating of the irrigation system and its associated sites as well as insights into one of the few ancient agricultural landscapes preserved in the Fayum.

Bibliography

Bonneau, M. 1979. "Un réglement de l'usage de l'eau au ve siècle." In *Hommages à la Mémoire de Serge Sauneron, 1927–1976*. Bibliothèque d'étude, 81. Cairo: Institut Français d'Archéologie Orientale, 2:3–23.

Bonneau, M. 1993. *Le régime administratif de l'eau du Nil dans l'Egypte grecque, romaine et byzantine*. Probleme der Ägyptologie, 8. Leiden and New York: E. J. Brill.

Boak, A. E. R. 1926. "Irrigation and Population in the Faiyum, the Garden of Egypt." *Geographical Review* 16.3:353–364.

Boak, A. E. R. 1955. "The Population of Roman and Byzantine Karanis." *Historia* 4:157–162.

Butzer, K. W. 1976. *Early Hydraulic Civilization in Egypt: A Study in Cultural Ecology*. Chicago: University of Chicago Press.

Caton-Thompson, G., and Gardner, E. W. 1934. *The Desert Fayum*. London: The Royal Anthropological Institute of Great Britain and Ireland.

Caton-Thompson, G., and Huzzayin, S. 1937. "Lake Moeris: Reinvestigations and Some Comments." *Bulletin de l'Institut d'Égypte* 19:243–303.

Keenan, J. G. 2003. "Deserted Villages: From the Ancient to the Medieval Fayyum." *Bulletin of the American Society of Papyrologists* 40:119–139.

Keenan, J. G. 2009. "The History of the Discipline." In R. Bagnall, ed., *The Oxford Handbook of Papyrology*. Oxford: Oxford University Press, 59–78.

Litinas, N. 2007. "*Habent sua fata fragmenta*: '*Donum Borgianum*'." In B. Palme, ed., *Akten des 23. Internationalen Papyrologenkongresses, Wien, 22.–28. Juli 2001*. Papyrologica Vindobonensia, 1. Vienna: Verlag der Österreichischen Akademie der Wissenschaften, 399–405.

Pollard, N. 1998. "The Chronology and Economic Condition of Late Roman Karanis: An Archaeological Reassessment." *Journal of the American Research Center in Egypt* 35:147–162.

Scarborough, V. L. 2003. *The Flow of Power: Ancient Water Systems and Landscapes*. Santa Fe: School for Advanced Research Press.

van Minnen, P. 1995. "Deserted Villages: Two Late Antique Town Sites in Egypt." *Bulletin of the American Society of Papyrologists* 32:41–56.

Excavating the Karanis Archives and Finding Magic in the Kelsey Museum

Andrew T. Wilburn

In antiquity, magic seldom was performed for the sake of entertainment: no rabbits were pulled from hats, nor were buildings rendered invisible. Instead, individuals turned to magic in order to address personal crises, such as easing a recurrent illness, winning a court case, or enticing a lover's affection. The Graeco-Roman Mediterranean was rife with magical solutions to individual dilemmas, which existed alongside, or even as part of, traditional religion. Through the analysis of artifacts and their archaeological contexts, the excavated material from Karanis offers a unique opportunity to situate magical practice in a local community.

We know quite a bit about the mechanics of magic in Greek and Roman Egypt, where the dry climate has preserved hundreds of documents on papyrus that attest to magical performance. These have been collected and are known as the *Greek Magical Papyri* and *Demotic Magical Papyri*, or *PGM* and *PDM*, respectively. These collections include a substantial number of ritual manuals that list the components of the rite, indicate how these materials are to be used, and specify what invocations the practitioner should intone. The magical papyri provide a veritable treasure trove of the sorts of items that could be magical: inscribed artifacts that bear spells or other words of power; figurines or other representations; the physical leavings of a victim, such as nail clippings or hair; plants, herbs, animals, or other natural substances; and household objects that were repurposed for magical use. These texts are immensely informative, but we must remember that the papyri are artifacts and should be associated with specific places and times, such as the Fayum, where Karanis was located.

Artifacts and papyri related to magic can enter the soil through a variety of circumstances: they may be lost or discarded, abandoned, or intentionally deposited. The close reading of an archaeological context may suggest that certain objects were deposited as part of a ritual. According to ancient documents, some spells would be effective only by placing the magical artifact in a specific place, sometimes in conjunction with other materials. Graves and cemeteries were often used for curses as these spaces permitted access to ghosts and underworld divinities.

Placement was also related to the goals of the rite: curse tablets related to chariot racing have been discovered in the circuses where races were held.

Finding Magic in the Michigan Excavations

The archival documents from the University of Michigan excavations at Karanis, currently housed in the Kelsey Museum, are instrumental for finding and understanding magical practices in the village. The Michigan team excavated houses and rooms, and used buildings to define the occupation phases at the site; all finds were catalogued according to the structure, room, and level in which they had been discovered and entered in the Record of Objects. Notation in the entries may provide further information about the circumstances of the finds, such as where in the soil the artifacts were discovered or whether certain artifacts were found all together. This level of detail permits us to associate finds with one another and with their archaeological contexts, although some problems do arise with stratigraphy (see articles by Cook, Gates-Foster, and Wilburn on pp. 157–160 below and Landvatter on pp. 39–43 it above).

A close reading of the Record of Objects can reveal the presence of unusual, weird, or strange objects and groups of objects. The archaeological context of "Objects of Interest" can be reconstructed by analyzing the maps and plans that were produced on site. Moreover, the excavation team made great use of photography, taking pictures of buildings and even objects as they were being excavated; these data, too, provide crucial information about finds and findspots. Careful analysis of the records that we do possess can yield profitable results, allowing us to reconstruct the processes that resulted in the deposition of an artifact. This, in turn, may permit us to suggest that individual objects or groups of objects were used in a ritual.

A number of other objects featured in the exhibition can be associated with magic rites through both their form and archaeological context. Some of these objects are clearly magical in nature: the papyrus amulet (object **74** above) is inscribed with a spell intended to ward off a fever from a man named Sarapion. Other artifacts require more circumspect analysis to uncover their magical function.

Magical Artifacts and Archaeological Contexts from Karanis

Found in the basement level of structure 165, a building that was part of an insula block on the eastern side of the settlement, a crude representation of a woman (object **72** above) was likely used in an aggressive erotic spell. The back of the head

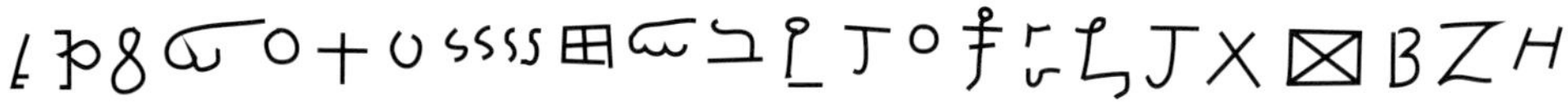

Fig. 54. Detail of a magical papyrus attributed to the Fayum region. The papyrus (PGM XXXVI = *P.Oslo* I.1) is a formulary that includes numerous spells for a variety of purposes, including inducing erotic attraction or harming an enemy. This section, part of a spell to create an amulet for favor or health (lines 275–283), includes symbols that are similar to those found on the bones.

of the doll appears to have been burned, likely by placing the doll into a fire. Spells from the magical papyri frequently use fire or heat in order to induce erotic attraction. For example, a spell may urge a practitioner to place a piece of papyrus in a hot bath and recite the incantation "TOU SETH, as you are in flames and on fire, so also [enflame] the soul, the heart of her, [name of victim], whom [name of victim's mother] bore, until she comes loving me, [name of commissioner]." Burning could also cause pain in the victim, suffering that would only be alleviated when the target of the spell came to the commissioner of the spell. The figurine was discovered in association with three bone pins; the point of one pin fits the eyehole of the figurine, suggesting that it may have been used to pierce the doll and induce pain. This group of artifacts was discovered beneath the house, which may suggest that it was placed here in order to draw the victim to the home of the commissioner.

On the northern side of the Karanis mound, excavators unearthed a stunning group of more than 84 fragments of animal bones and objects that were similar in appearance to the bones (object **135** above). All of these objects had been painted with red ocher in one or more of three designs: dots, lines, or undulating lines. Some of the marks on the bones are similar to symbols of power known from the magical papyri (fig. 54). Even if the designs do not make letters or words, they may reflect the desire of an individual to inscribe mystical markings on these objects. Among the spells of the papyri, bones are named in rites for protection, for harnessing the power of the dead, and were used to record medical prescriptions.

The bones would have been recognizable as belonging to animals, which may suggest that they were used for problems with livestock. In the magical papyri and on magical gems, the line pattern is associated with health and protection (fig. 55). So, too, the dot pattern perhaps may be related to well-being, either by representing the appearance of healthy, living animals with spots or, conversely, sickly animals that are afflicted with boils, pustules, or other physical defects. While there is little evidence for pastoral concerns in the *PGM/PDM*, a healing rite attributed to the

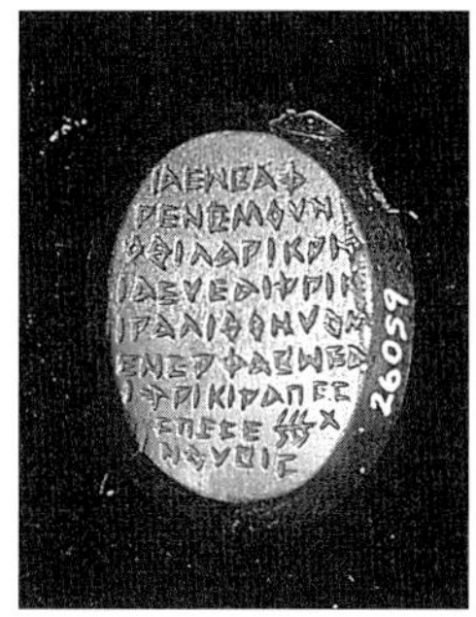

Fig. 55. Reverse of magical amulet made of haematite, purchased in Egypt. The inscription includes a series of magical words. At the end of the inscription, the Greek phrase, "Digest! Digest!" precedes a symbol of three undulating lines bisected by a horizontal line and the name of the god Chnoubis. The amulet likely was intended to ease indigestion (KM 26059.).

Egyptian Bolus of Mendes urges the shepherd to bury one animal upside-down at the gate to the pen and drive the other sheep over it (Wilburn 2012, 157 and n. 176). In this way, illness was drawn from the living animals into the dead one. The bones may have been used in a similar fashion, as talismans meant to draw off sickness or impart health to diseased herds.

Objects such as the figurine of a woman or the painted bones are similar to the materials listed in the spell instructions of the magical papyri, but they do not precisely meet our expectations. Practitioners likely took liberties with the spells that they consulted, and we certainly do not possess written records for all of the magical spells that may have been performed. We are best served by using the *Greek Magical Papyri* as a rough guide for how magic was performed in antiquity, providing insight into the sorts of rituals that may have been performed and the classes of materials that were used. These data can be compared to evidence that comes out of the ground; findspots and archaeological context can tell us about the processes that led to the deposition of magical objects. Indeed, to discover what the performance of rituals looked like within an individual community, we must rely on archaeological evidence, the only data source that can be associated securely with a specific town, village, or region.

Bibliography

Bailliot, M. 2010. *Magie et sortilèges dans l'Antiquité romaine*. Paris: Hermann.

Betz, H. D. 1992. *The Greek Magical Papyri in Translation*. Chicago: University of Chicago Press.

Bohak, G. 2008. *Ancient Jewish Magic: A History*. New York: Cambridge University Press.

Dieleman, J. 2005. *Priests, Tongues, and Rites: The London-Leiden Magical Manuscripts and Translation in Egyptian Ritual (100–300 CE)*. Leiden: Brill.

Faraone, C. A. 1999. *Ancient Greek Love Magic*. Cambridge: Cambridge University Press.

Faraone, C. A., and Obbink, D. 1991. *Magika Hiera: Ancient Greek Magic and Religion*. New York: Oxford University Press.

Frankfurter, D. 1998. *Religion in Roman Egypt: Assimilation and Resistance*. Princeton: Princeton University Press.

Gager, J. G. 1992. *Curse Tablets and Binding Spells from Antiquity and the Ancient World*. New York: Oxford University Press.

Graf, F. 1997. *Magic in the Ancient World*. Cambridge: Cambridge University Press.

Wilburn, A. T. 2012. *Materia Magica: The Archaeology of Magic in Roman Egypt, Cyprus, and Spain*. New Texts from Ancient Cultures. Ann Arbor: University of Michigan Press.

The Karanis Housing Project: A New Approach to an Old Excavation

Andrew T. Wilburn, R. James Cook, and Jennifer Gates-Foster

From the Past

Excavation of a house at Karanis in the 1924–1925 season unearthed a small, rather mundane scrap of papyrus (P.Mich.inv. 4604, object **111** above; Litinas and Cook forthcoming). Dating to the early 5th century AD, this innocuous text is a receipt for the delivery of grain for tax purposes. By itself the receipt is neither unique nor particularly informative, but recognizing that the papyrus was excavated at Karanis allows us to draw important conclusions about the inhabitants of the site in the later years of the settlement.

For example, the latest datable papyrus mentioning Karanis, *P. Haun* III 58, records the resolution of a water dispute involving the inhabitants of the village over an otherwise unknown place called Thanesamen in the year AD 439 (Rea 1993, with earlier bibliography). Its ambiguous phrasing has compromised interpretation of this difficult text, leading one scholar to question which individuals were resident in Karanis and which in Thanesamen (van Minnen 1995, 51 n. 46). The Michigan document records the payment of tax on behalf of Karanis by Atesios, son of Paulos, one of the individuals mentioned in the water dispute. The fact that the receipt was *excavated* from a house at Karanis suggests that Atesios lived there, rather than at or near Thanesamen, and provides additional proof that the site was actively occupied and used as a tax center in the 5th century AD.

The vast majority of papyri in collections around the world, like *P. Haun* III 58, the ambiguous water dispute, were purchased from dealers and lack secure provenance. The absence of context limits the types of questions that may be asked of the documents as well as our ability to interpret them. In contrast, the artifacts and papyri discovered at Karanis can be associated with relatively precise findspots and contexts. The University of Michigan excavations achieved a level of documentation unparalleled at the time, and the archival material in the Kelsey Museum of Archaeology and the University of Michigan Papyrus Collection provides a unique resource for reconstructing the original artifact assemblages from an early scientific excavation within their architectural settings. The Karanis Housing Project attempts to begin this process through a targeted study. The primary objective of this collaborative project is to recontextualize the finds from a few select buildings in their entirety, integrating the study of texts and artifacts within a circumscribed architectural environment.

Toward the Future

Over the past 25 years, there have been numerous calls to reintegrate the study of texts and artifacts (van Minnen 1994; Gagos, Gates, and Wilburn 2005). Despite the frequency of such demands for action, there have been few attempts to fully incorporate papyri and objects in print or other publications. In part, this reticence can be traced to the belief that papyri and artifacts tell us different things. An inscribed receipt, such as the papyrus mentioned above, is clear about its owner and function, while the remains of the granary and the grain to which it refers provide a very different type of evidence. But, as the late Traianos Gagos, the archivist of the Papyrus Collection at the University of Michigan and an associate research scientist in the Kelsey Museum, frequently reminded his students and colleagues, a papyrus itself is an artifact, with a unique findspot and context. Indeed, this context has much to tell us about how the papyrus was used, at least at one point in its material life, and its nature as a physical artifact. Conversely, the contents of the papyrus may inform us about the residents of a specific home, or about the chronology of a building, but also offer insight into the materiality of textual production.

The publication of papyri from excavations has suffered the same fate as many other classes of material evidence. Excavation produces massive quantities of artifacts, and no single individual possesses sufficient expertise in all of the requisite fields. Classes of data, such as coins or faunal remains, typically are published by specialists in separate chapters of a single volume. This dispersal of material often clouds our understanding of individual archaeological contexts by obscuring the associations among different types of objects that were deposited and possibly used in the same place at the same time. This material may have much to tell us about ancient individuals at the site.

The Karanis Housing Project will attempt to produce a unified synthesis of all the finds associated with a small, select number of buildings on the site, understood diachronically through the various occupation phases. The size of the site (and the quantity of excavated material) makes it difficult to fully appreciate the complexities of the village. By beginning with smaller units, we hope to suggest patterns of occupation that can be tested against other areas of the site. Building upon GIS work completed by Andrew Wilburn, the architecture of selected buildings will be reconstructed virtually, using computer software, and each artifact and text will be placed inside. Reconstructing the buildings and their contents will allow us to comprehend how single houses and structures at the site were built, inhabited, and fell into disrepair. We hope to get a sense of how our chosen buildings were used, who lived within them, and how they (the structures and residents) interacted with their neighbors. The ultimate objective of the project is the creation of the first synthetic study that fully integrates archaeological and papyrological evidence to reconstruct the lived and experienced environment, as understood through a few individual buildings.

Just as contemporary interdisciplinary archaeological excavations require the participation of numerous specialists, so the reconstruction of contexts from past excavations benefits from collaborative enterprise. The Karanis Project team gathers archaeologists and papyrologists to work together at every stage of the process, from identifying suitable areas for investigation to analyzing the data and producing a final publication.

Conclusion

The study of earlier excavations is complicated, particularly when the individuals who oversaw the fieldwork have passed away. Although we may lack their firsthand testimony, we do possess detailed records from the field. Indeed, solely by virtue of its recordkeeping, the Michigan excavations at Karanis employed methodologies far ahead of their contemporaries. This vital source of information, currently housed in the Kelsey Museum, provides an unparalleled and priceless glimpse into the past and serves as the basis for a collaborative, interdisciplinary project that applies evolving theoretical perspectives to the material culture of Karanis.

Bibliography

Gagos, T., Gates, J. E., and Wilburn, A. 2005. "Material Culture and Texts of Graeco-Roman Egypt: Creating Context, Debating Meaning." *Bulletin of the American Society of Papyrologists* 42:171–188.

Keenan, J. G. 2003. "Deserted Villages: From the Ancient to the Medieval Fayum." *Bulletin of the American Society of Papyrologists* 40:119–139.

Litinas, N., and Cook, R. J. Forthcoming. "A Fifth Century Receipt for the Delivery of Wheat from Karanis (P.Mich.inv. 4604)." *Archiv für Papyrusforschung.*

Nevett, L. 2011. "Family and Household, Ancient History and Archeology: A Case Study from Roman Egypt." In *A Companion to Families in the Greek and Roman Worlds*, ed. B. Rawson. Oxford: Wiley-Blackwell, 15–31.

Rea, J. 1993. "P.Haun. III 58: Caranis in the Fifth Century." *Zeitschrift für Papyrologie und Epigraphik* 99:89–95.

van Minnen, P. 1994. "House-to-House Enquiries: An Interdisciplinary Approach to Roman Karanis." *Zeitschrift für Papyrologie und Epigraphik* 100:227–251.

van Minnen, P. 1995. "Deserted Villages: Two Late Antique Town Sites in Egypt." *Bulletin of the American Society of Papyrologists* 32:41–56.

The Threshold Papyri from Karanis

W. Graham Claytor

The image of worm-eaten rolls lying within a wooden threshold has often been reproduced, and indeed has become somewhat of a symbol for the prospect of integrating papyrological and archaeological evidence (fig. 56).[1] The contents of these papyri from Karanis, however, have not been clearly laid out in print, and only two texts have been published to date. This note establishes which papyri were found in the threshold and argues that they belonged to the manager of Karanis's *grapheion* (writing office) in the early 2nd century AD.

First, credit is due to Philip Deloria, who made an accurate identification of the threshold texts in an undergraduate honors thesis;[2] to Traianos Gagos and Nikolaos Litinas, who reexamined the unpublished texts for Deloria; and to Orsamus Pearl, whose preliminary transcriptions of some of these texts can be consulted in the Michigan Papyrology Collection.[3] The discussion below is based on their observations and my own work on the papyri in the Michigan collection.

The published summary of excavation reports states that in house (C)5026,[4] "the outer threshold beam of the door between rooms D and E has been hollowed out and in that space had been concealed several papyrus documents of the first half of the second century." A footnote reveals that these are P.Mich.inv. 4388–91 (Husselman 1979, 15 and n. 20). This identification of the threshold papyri is traceable back to the unpublished Karanis excavation report by Enoch Peterson.[5]

[1] For the latest discussion of papyri in their archaeological context, see Verhoogt 2012. I thank Prof. Verhoogt for an advance copy of his article.

[2] Deloria published a summary of this thesis in the *Kelsey Museum Newsletter* (Spring 2005), 6–7.

[3] Pearl, boxes 1 and 3, University of Michigan Papyrus Collection, 807 Hatcher Library.

[4] The "C" refers to the later assignment of this house to the stratigraphic layer C. For a discussion of the difficulties with the stratigraphy of Karanis, see Stephan and Verhoogt 2005, 191–196.

[5] Described above on pp. 20–22; see pp. 100 and 865 of the Peterson report.

Fig. 56. Threshold papyri as found (Kelsey Museum neg. no. 5.1801).

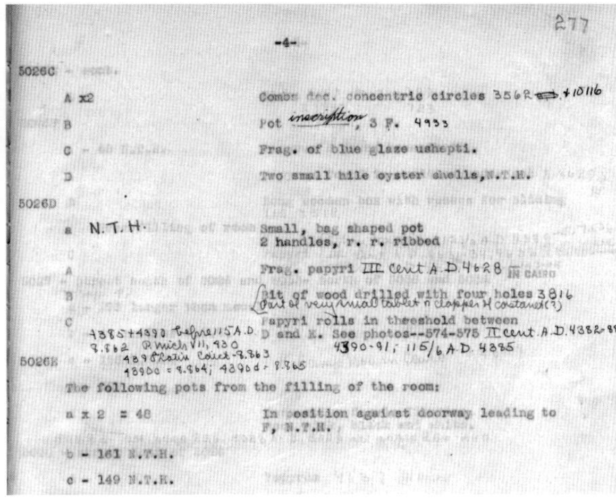

Fig. 57. Record of Objects Book entry for structure 5026, room D.

But the Record of Objects, held in the Kelsey Museum of Archaeology, introduces a discrepancy. There, under field number 5026D-C,[6] we read: "Papyri rolls in threshold between D and E," followed by excavation director Enoch Peterson's handwritten note in red ink giving the inventory numbers 4382–88 and 4390–91 (see fig. 57). Somehow, in compiling the excavations reports, this information was overlooked or misinterpreted, and the threshold papyri became associated with inv. 4388–91. The accidental inclusion of 4389 (= *P.Mich.* IX 551), which was actually found in a nearby room,[7] is explicable by its position in this series of inventory numbers, but the exclusion of 4382–87 is difficult to explain.

Connections among the texts in this series were actually noticed long ago: *P.Mich.* VII 430, a collection of Latin sayings, consists of fragments from inv. 4385 and 4390. This papyrus was later pasted together with a report of land inspection (*episkepsis*, P.*Congr.* XV 15) to form a long roll for use in Karanis's *grapheion*. A scribe, perhaps even the manager of the *grapheion*, used this newly formed roll to write a day-by-day register (*anagraphe*) of documents drawn up in the *grapheion*. This register records the writing fee (*grammatikon*) paid for drawing up each document, which means it was a private financial document belonging to the manager of the *grapheion*.

[6] This field number can be parsed as: the third find (C) recorded in room D of structure 5026.

[7] Room F (25-5026F-C). This contract records the sale of a donkey to the veteran Gaius Valerius Longus. See now Vanbeselaere 2013.

This type of document is best paralleled by *P.Mich.* II 123 recto, covering receipts of the writing fee in the village of Tebtunis's *grapheion* in AD 45–46, with accounts of expenditures on the other side. The Karanis text, however, incorporates expenditures into the structure of the register and diligently balances these expenditures against the receipts of the writing fee on a daily and periodic basis. It can thus be seen as a hybrid and streamlined version of the Tebtunis roll.

Of the other fragments in the series 4382–88 and 4390–91, all except one clearly preserve columns of this same register on their versos. The outlier, 4388, is a magical or astronomical text that at first glance appears to have little to do with the *grapheion*. One side, however, was washed clean, and I suggest that it was introduced into the archive for eventual reuse, just like the sheet of Latin sayings and the report of land inspection.

Far from a multifunctional archive, therefore, the threshold texts were all assembled by a frugal *grapheion* manager for the single purpose of balancing his checkbook. I am undertaking further study of the register, which will give us a more detailed picture of social and economic life in the village of Karanis, while a full study of all the papyrological and archaeological evidence from house 5026 would provide a better context for these *grapheion* texts.

Appendix. The Threshold Papyri, Karanis

P.Mich.inv. #	*Recto*	*Verso*
4382	*anagraphe**	Karanis *anagraphe*
4383	Two different *episkepseis* pasted together	Karanis *anagraphe*
4384	*episkepsis*	Karanis *anagraphe*
4385	*episkepsis* (*P.Congr.* XV) and Latin sayings (*P.Mich.* VII 430)	Karanis *anagraphe*
4386	*episkepsis*	Karanis *anagraphe*
4387	*episkepsis* and *anagraphe*	Karanis *anagraphe*
4388	washed clean	magical or astronomical text
4390	Latin sayings (*P.Mich.* VII 430)	Karanis *anagraphe*
4391	*episkepsis*	Karanis *anagraphe*

* Interestingly, this *anagraphe* is written in a different hand from that found on the versos of the threshold papyri. This same hand is found on the recto of inv. 4387, where it is pasted to a sheet from an *episkepsis*. Clearly, then, this is an older *anagraphe* that the Karanis *grapheion* manager incorporated into his recycled rolls.

Bibliography

Husselman, E. M. 1979. *Karanis Excavations of the University of Michigan in Egypt 1928–1935: Topography and Architecture. A Summary of the Reports of the Director, Enoch E. Peterson*. Kelsey Museum of Archaeology Studies, 5. Ann Arbor: University of Michigan Press.

Stephan, R. P., and Verhoogt, A. 2005. "Text and Context in the Archive of Tiberianus." *Bulletin of the American Society of Papyrologists* 42:191–196.

Vanbeselaere, S. 2013. "The Gaii Valerii. Gaius Valerius Longus' Alleged Archive and His Relatives." *Zeitschrift für Papyrologie und Epigraphik* 187:239–262.

Verhoogt, A. 2012. "Papyri in the Archaeological Record." In C. Riggs, ed., *The Oxford Handbook of Roman Egypt*. Oxford: Oxford University Press, 507–515.

Reconstructing the Contexts of a Greek Musical Papyrus from Karanis

Rebecca A. Sears

In my 2012 dissertation, titled "The Practical Muse: Reconstructing the Contexts of a Greek Musical Papyrus," I undertake an extensive reexamination of the recto of P.Mich.inv. 2958, a 2nd-century AD musical papyrus excavated by the University of Michigan at Karanis (Kom Aushim) in the Fayum, Egypt, in 1924 (fig. 58). Although this papyrus has a significant publication history, the text continues to present editors with challenging textual and interpretive questions. In my investigation of this papyrus, I utilize methodological approaches from a variety of disciplines, including papyrology, musicology, and archaeology, in order to contextualize the physical document as well as the text and notation that it preserves. My research emphasizes the evidence this unique papyrus can provide concerning non-elite Greek musical practices in Roman Egypt during the 2nd century AD and further discusses how this papyrus relates to the writings of the ancient Greek musical theorists. From this investigation, I conclude that P.Mich.inv. 2958 represents a rare example of community-oriented, professional (or semiprofessional) musicianship and demonstrates that high-quality music-making was not restricted to the hyper-elite contexts of courts, cities, and the major pan-Hellenic festivals.

My study initially focuses on the excavation context of this papyrus, represented through the field number 24-5006E^2-A, and on reconstructing a provisional impression of the musical community of the Fayum in the early to middle Roman period. This papyrus belongs to a large group of diverse papyri, more than 136 inventory numbers, found in the same archaeological context, including the approximately 39 documentary papyri of the archive of Gemellus Horion—also known as the archive of Gaius Apol(l)inarius Niger. Therefore, this papyrus is one of a very few musical documents that can be associated with other papyri, even if only through its reuse as an account. I then turn to an examination of other papyri, ostraka, and even fragments of musical instruments in order to reconstruct some sense of the musical milieu of the Fayum. On the basis of this evidence, I conclude that, despite the rural, agricultural character of the region, musical performance formed an integral part of social activities in this mixed Egyptian, Greek, and Roman community.

Fig. 58. P. Mich.inv. 2958, recto (photograph courtesy of the University of Michigan Library Papyrology Collection).

I then present a re-edition of the text and notation (*semeia*), along with an *apparatus criticus* and substantial commentary discussing alternative readings of both aspects of the papyrus. Although there have been three previous editions, the generally poor preservation of the papyrus has created significant obstacles to the establishment of secure textual and musical readings. The presence of the *semeia* further complicates reading the papyrus for a variety of reasons, including the irregular spacing of the text, which problematizes textual reconstruction by occluding the number of letters missing in a lacuna, the occasional confusion of the textual and musical registers, and the difficulty in determining what a "correct" reading of the musical line might entail. While the possible interpretations of a damaged character in the text are restricted by the known language (Greek), the limited information on Greek melodic practices hinders parallel determinations for the *semeia*. I then offer a translation of the musical notation of P.Mich.inv. 2958 into modern Western notation with its realization in sound (in WAV format), created through the musical composition software Finale; a second arrangement intended for modern performance, with an accompanying recording of a reading of that transcription; and finally, a discussion of the problems inherent in and the techniques required for such reconstructions.

I subsequently offer a musicological commentary discussing certain aspects of the notation, including the relationship of this papyrus to surviving theoretical treatises. I focus on a metrical and rhythmic analysis, a close examination of the melismata, a discussion of cadential patterns, two specific examples of text setting, and finally, the technique of modulation (*metabolē*). Through this discussion, I demonstrate that even though the literary merits of the text may be dubious, the musical score is both sophisticated and nearly unparalleled in the extant corpus of Greek musical documents. The sophisticated use of the Greek vocal notation system, including the extensive use of rhythmic signs and other performance markings, supports the idea that P.Mich.inv. 2958 comes from a professional context and may well have been used in a performance situation.

Finally, I explore several theories about the possible use contexts of P.Mich.inv. 2958. In this discussion, I examine the question of the authorship of the papyrus in relation to the composition of both text and music through the reconstruction of two hypothetical scenarios. Then I draw upon the Karanis material, as well as some new evidence from other Graeco-Roman musical settings, in order to recreate several contexts in which P.Mich.inv. 2958 may have been used by professional Greek musicians in Egypt. This discussion is intensely hypothetical, although nevertheless based on the evidence gathered through the avenues of research presented above. I offer these suggestions as a thought experiment designed to provoke a reexamination of the customary scholarly assumptions about the musical papyri, namely that all or most of the musical papyri originated in Alexandria in the hyper-elite contexts found in that metropolis.

I continue to pursue research closely related to this dissertation since the scope of the project did not permit the detailed examination of every interesting feature of P.Mich.inv. 2958. In addition to the projected publication of my re-edition of this papyrus, I am focusing on the inherent interdisciplinary potential of the musical papyri. In particular, I would like to raise greater awareness of the resources for the study of ancient Greek music among musicologists, who have largely remained unaware of the surviving material, through writing a series of articles based on my melodic analysis of P.Mich.inv. 2958. Furthermore, I intend to continue researching the relationship of the musical papyri to the Egyptian communities in which they were found, especially through a more detailed analysis of the musical instruments found in Karanis. While I presented a brief discussion of these in my dissertation, further research is certainly warranted and will hopefully provide greater insight into the interaction and mutual influence of both the Greek and Egyptian musical cultures. These ongoing projects all emphasize the potential for musical documents to permeate boundaries ingrained into our own academic culture.

In conclusion, the musical significance of P.Mich.inv. 2958 should not be understated: this papyrus presents a rare and valuable window into the practical relationship of musical theory, composition, and performance in Graeco-Roman Egypt. Although most studies concerning ancient Greek music focus on the development of musical practices in the Archaic period and their culmination during the Classical period, much of our evidence, both theoretical and papyrological, comes from the Hellenistic and Roman periods. The musical sensitivity and complexity of this fragment challenges the perceived decline of Greek music from the Classical ideals of 5th-century Athens and instead signifies a differing aesthetic, one that may well have influenced the development of early Christian chant and, therefore, the course of Western musical history.

The Sonic Landscape of Karanis: Excavating the Sounds of a Village in Roman Egypt

T. G. Wilfong

Sound is an integral part of most human experience, but the study of the ancient world rarely takes sound into account: apart from ancient music, the sonic environments of ancient cultures have received little scholarly attention. The soundscapes of the ancient world are a rich potential source for investigation, however, and the methodologies of modern cultural historians who study sound can provide new insight into ancient cultures. The Michigan excavations at Karanis yielded a wide variety of material that can reveal much about the sonic landscapes of this ancient village, and, although still at a relatively early stage, my own research in this area has resulted in a cluster of projects centering on the sounds of Karanis.

The tendency in historical scholarship has been to equate the study of sound in the past with the study of music, and indeed my own work on sound at Karanis has its origins in material relating to music. The Michigan excavations at Karanis uncovered a wide range of musical instruments and related artifacts, as well as papyri pertaining to ancient music. The Michigan expedition recovered percussion instruments such as bells, castanets, clappers, wind instruments, including whistles, flutes, and fragments of at least two substantial bronze auloi, as well as toys (buzzers and baby rattles, one of the latter being a basketry rattle containing noisemakers consisting of shards of glass) and a group of bone plectra for stringed instruments. Relevant papyri include the well-known fragment of musical notation (P.Mich. inv. 2958, discussed above on pp. 165–168) and a set of rules for a musical contest involving flute and kithara players (P.Mich.inv. 4682). Moreover, the archaeological contexts of the material suggest relationships and connections between the relatively uncommon artifacts of music and the wider culture of Karanis: the domestic findspots of the papyrus with musical notation and the musical contest rules may say something about the presence of professional musicians in the town, while the find of a group of castanets stored with valuable domestic goods found in structure

209 may indicate the presence of castanet dancers in this particular household.[1] A preliminary overview of this material appeared in the 1999 Kelsey Museum exhibition "Music in Roman Egypt."[2]

Relatively little work has been done on the musical instruments and material culture of music in Roman Egypt, especially in comparison to the amount of attention devoted to the surviving fragments of musical notation from Roman Egypt and attempts to reconstruct the music they present. Indeed, previous work on the music of Karanis has centered almost exclusively on the reconstruction and interpretation of the musical notation for a dialogue concerning Orestes in P.Mich.inv. 2958: In addition to the *editio princeps* (Pearl and Winnington-Ingram 1965), and the treatments of the notation (recently in Pöhlmann and West 2001), the papyrus has been the object of a recent dissertation (Sears 2012).[3] Moreover, at least three commercially available recordings bear witness to attempts to reconstruct and play the music notated in the papyrus.[4] These widely differing takes on ancient music based on papyrological evidence show something of the challenges facing any would-be interpreter of this music: tempo, instrumentation, and other factors are uncertain, and the gaps left by the fragmentary nature of all papyri containing musical notation add further difficulties.[5] For musicians and even for musically

[1] Although the circumstances of the find are similar to the one described above (pp. 87–92), and one cannot rule out the possibility of the castanets' being part of a woodworker's stock, the circumstances of their caching with valuable glass and other items suggest instead the storage of a household's valuables against an intended return to collect them.

[2] See the exhibition website at http://lw.lsa.umich.edu/kelsey/galleries/Exhibits/MIRE/MIRE.html; musicologist Christopher Dempsey has prepared technical descriptions of most of the Karanis instruments toward an eventual publication of the material.

[3] This work, and the author's intended future direction, is summarized in her essay above.

[4] "Papyrus Michigan" [Track 9] in Atrium Musicae de Madrid 1979; "Fragment of Orestie" [Track 9] in Ensemble Kérylos 1996; and "Tragic Dialogue on Orestes: Papyrus Michigan inv. 2958" [Track 20] in De Organographia 1995. Note also the reconstructions prepared by Rebecca Sears for her dissertation cited above, available online at: http://deepblue.lib.umich.edu/handle/2027.42/90511.

[5] Performers of this music have dealt with the issue of lacunae in the notation in various ways; the missing music can be skipped or reconstructed, the approach of Ensemble Kérylos and De Organographia, or the gaps can be indicated, even emphasized, as in the Atrium Musicae de Madrid reconstructions, where lacunae and breaks in the texts are marked with periods of dissonance or noise.

Fig. 59. A group of bronze bells, found in area CS48 (Kelsey Museum neg. no. 5.2603).

inclined archaeologists and historians, the reconstruction, performance, and recording of music from ancient notation can be a satisfying, creative endeavor but carries considerable risks of anachronism and the imposition of modern musical ideas and approaches onto the ancients.[6] For an understanding of the place of music in the world of Roman Egypt, attempting the reconstruction of ancient music may finally be a distraction that obscures more interesting and ultimately more answerable questions about the contexts and functions of music in Roman Egypt that are better supported by the surviving evidence.

Work on the Karanis musical instruments further raises questions of the complexities of defining music and the limitations that this imposes on inquiry: although we categorize many of the Karanis instruments as "musical" because of their functions in our own culture, their actual uses at Karanis were intended to produce not music but rather sound. So the many bronze bells found at Karanis, for example, can in one sense be categorized as musical instruments but would have been used in nonmusical ways, most often as bells for animals in farming contexts (fig. 59). Likewise, the sound-producing toys, the rattles, clappers, buzzers, and even whistles, might be characterized as musical but were much more likely

[6] Note the remarks of Assyriologist (and musician) Piotr Michalowski, who characterizes attempts at reconstruction of ancient Near Eastern music as "a pursuit that may be harmless, but is, to my mind at least, nothing but folly" (Michalowski 2010, 117).

intended as noisemakers. An exclusive focus on music at Karanis would therefore miss many opportunities provided by these instruments for understanding the wider sonic world of Karanis, and indeed music itself has to be understood in its wider sonic context.

And so the shift in emphasis of my project from music to wider questions of sound at Karanis began, promising a potentially much more interesting and fruitful area of investigation. This transition was aided by other unrelated projects that attested to the importance of sound and the often unlikely sources for its study. A casual question in connection with a Kelsey Museum exhibition on animals in the ancient world, for example, led to an investigation of culturally specific renderings of animal noises in Egyptian texts (often reflected in the Egyptian words for the animals themselves).[7] In another context, working on papyri containing funerary texts of the pharaonic and Graeco-Roman periods revealed a world of nonmusical sound in recurring references to noise and sound in the Egyptian afterlife. Graeco-Roman period funerary texts, for example, contain repeated references to the wailing and lamentations heard in the afterlife.[8] Even more striking are the range of sounds evoked in the pharaonic Book of Amduat: note in particular the Eighth Hour, in which the Netherworld gods respond to the calls of the sun-god in mysterious voices likened to the buzzing of bees, the laments of humans, the mating calls of bulls, pleadings of great force, the cries of male cats, the murmuring of the living, the sound of a riverbank falling into the watery abyss, the cry of a divine falcon, and the sounds of a nest of birds, and these sounds, although incomprehensible to humans as speech, are said to illuminate the darkness and cause the sun-god to rejoice.[9] Indeed, sounds are invoked throughout the text, suggesting an environment punctuated by sound, as the sun-god moves through on his nightly progress. Clearly, for the Egyptians, sound was a significant part of their understanding of the unseen realms of the dead and the gods—the nature of the sounds and their descriptions suggest landscapes pervaded by anxiety and unease. And even the sounds of the daily life activities depicted in elite tombs are described: note the

[7] For example, note the Middle Egyptian words for "cat" *miw*, "lion" *m3w*, "dog" *iwiw*, and the sounds made by a cow (*nmi*) and a goose (*g3g3*).

[8] These texts are translated in Smith 2009; note in particular the ritual wailing punctuated by stamping of feet (79 and discussion at 69 and n. 13).

[9] Translated in Hornung 1989, 140–151, and note Hornung's own summary in Hornung 1999, 39–40.

extraordinary "appeal to the living" from the Theban tomb of Ibi, in which the tomb visitor is asked to hear the sounds of the workers quarreling, the musicians playing, and the mourners wailing.[10] The simple fact that they have taken the time to describe the soundscape so vividly suggests that it is worth further study.[11]

A very different project produced what was, for me, perhaps the most striking example of the significance of sound and its potential for research—a reference encountered in my investigation of the discourse of homoerotic relations in Late Antique Egypt, drawn primarily from hostile invective in Coptic monastic sources—and this case is perhaps worth discussion at some greater length here. An unusual homily attributed to the 5th-century AD monk Horsiesios described, from a hostile perspective, what can only be seen as a covert subculture of monks involved in homosexual relationships and does so partly in terms of sound. Indeed, the sounds that these monks make help Horsiesios identify them as a distinct group and differentiate them from the other monks:

> Now, some from your (circle of) friendship go out with their faces shaved, wearing veils around their faces and throwing on a black thing over their eyes with the excuse of illness. They tie multitudes of rings to their handkerchiefs, and fringes come down behind them from their belt, like calves jumping around in an enclosure. [. . .] Light sandals on their feet—"She went out taking pride in the desire of her soul"—they clatter with their feet in the midst of the assembly. They greet their friend with high laughter, like the sound of thorn-branches burning under the cauldron.[12]

Horsiesios uses negative associations of sound to reinforce the negativity of his description of this monastic group he dislikes, but the sounds also serve to highlight his anxiety about their existence and activities—not unlike the anxiety invoked in the much earlier Netherworld noises in the Book of Amduat. In particular, his comparison of the monks' laughter to the sound of burning thorn-branches crackling under a cauldron is most striking: Horsiesios relies on phonomnesis (a sound imagined in memory but not physically heard) here. And

[10] See the brief description in Hartwig 2011 and references therein; thanks to Janet Richards for this reference.

[11] Note the study of the related concept of hearing in the Netherworld: Wiebach-Koepke 2003.

[12] Translation Wilfong 2002, 315.

surely this is comparable to the modern (although disappearing) evocation of fingernails on a chalkboard—a negative sound that evokes a visceral reaction just by its mention. David Toop has discussed the haunting effects of sound through the use of text to conjure up memories of sound,[13] and I think that is part of Horsiesios's strategy here.

For my own purposes, not only does this passage invoke sounds through verbal descriptions, but it also invites connection to the surviving material culture of the time. The jangling of the rings on the handkerchiefs may not have precise parallels in the archaeological record, but those "light sandals" that "clatter" would have been similar to the many, roughly contemporary, palm fiber sandals retrieved from the Michigan excavations at Karanis. The sounds they would have made would have been affected, at least in part, by the floor surfaces they struck—dirt, mud-brick, or stone. And surely the monks' "high laughter" would have sounded different in different environments, raising questions about monastic architecture and materials.[14]

In all of these cases, work in a variety of areas kept coming back to this issue of sound in the ancient world, and this recurrence of the importance of sound reinforced the idea of using the Karanis material to go beyond the study of music and investigate wider questions of sonic environments at Karanis from the archaeological and textual evidence. There is no real precedent in the study of the ancient Mediterranean world for such an inquiry, however, and this work proved difficult to begin. The wider study of sound, although as yet far from extensive, is of increasing interest to a range of cultural and intellectual historians, and their work can provide a valuable theoretical underpinning to work on sound in the ancient world.[15] Many of the studies coming out in this area begin, as did the cases described above, with textual reference to sound, and this seemed to be a logical beginning point for looking at the Karanis material. But the richness of the material culture and the rare bonus of having such material from a secure and complex archaeological

[13] Note Toop 2010, especially at 127–177. Thanks to John Kannenberg for the reference as well as for his observations on this text, of which I have made free use here.

[14] Particularly relevant in Horsiesios's homily when he discusses the monks' use of architectural features in the monastery for hiding things.

[15] Note, for example, the classic work *The Soundscape* (Schafer 1993) and the overview of recent work in Bull and Back 2004.

context seemed to call for a focus on the artifactual evidence, or at least to use this material as a starting point.

This artifact-based approach received valuable impetus from a meeting with artist John Kannenberg, who approached me about advice for his trip to Egypt to make field recordings at a number of sites, including Karanis (described in his article below on pp. 179–181). It soon became clear that we shared many interests in sound and archaeology, the interrelationships of artifacts and sound, and also the roles and places of sound in museums. Our discussions of these shared interests have resulted in a number of collaborative efforts and have also given my own research in this area a better focus. Perhaps of greatest relevance to the present discussion is our collaboration on an open-storage display component curated by John for the Kelsey Museum Graeco-Roman Egypt gallery; this focus on objects coincided with my own concerns about using Karanis objects to understand Karanis sounds. Initially, this project was intended to adapt elements of my 1999 "Music in Roman Egypt" exhibition for the permanent gallery, but both of us found this concept too limiting and eventually expanded on the idea to illustrate more widely the sounds of Roman Egypt. To this end, John has chosen a wide range of artifacts from Karanis that would have produced sound in some way—a few musical instruments but also coins, glass fragments, a hammer, and even (in a nod to Horsiesios's homily) a sandal—as well as ancient representations of animals and other things that made sound at Karanis. John's installation will place an image of a Roman period Egyptian in the middle of the objects that make up his sonic environment, surrounded by the objects along with vivid word evocations of the sounds represented by the objects.

Beyond the immediate purposes of this open-storage display, the concentration on Karanis artifacts required for this museum installation (and the subsequent work on artifacts in preparation for the "Karanis Revealed" exhibition) has reinforced the idea of an object-centered approach to the problems of understanding the sonic landscape of Karanis. Taking advantage of the presence of objects and archival excavation records at the Kelsey Museum (and the relevant papyri at the University of Michigan Library Papyrology Collection), I hope to arrive at some understanding of the sonic environment of Karanis firmly grounded in the material culture and archaeology of the site. The ultimate outcome of such a study remains unclear, but it will be disseminated in some way other than a printed publication, possibly drawing on the concept of "museums of sound" being developed by John Kannenberg and the work that John and I are doing on the wider roles, uses, and manifestations of sound in museums. My goal is to present a virtual museum installation that draws on the Kelsey Museum Karanis material to transcend the boundaries of both a traditional publication and a conventional museum exhibition.

Bibliography

Atrium Musicae de Madrid 1979. *Musique de la Grèce antique/Ancient Greek Music/Griechische Musik der Antike*. Direction G. Paniagua. Audio CD. Harmonia Mundi France: HMA 1901015.

Bull, M., and Back, L. 2004. *The Auditory Culture Reader*. Sensory Formations Series. New York: Berg.

De Organographia 1995. *Music of the Ancient Greeks*. G. Stuwe Neuman, P. Neuman, and W. Gavin. Audio CD. Pandourion Records USA: PRCD1001.

Ensemble Kérylos 1996. *Musiques de l'Antiquité Grecque*. Direction A. Bélis. Audio CD. K617: K617069.

Hartwig, M. 2011. "An Examination of Art Historical Method and Theory: A Case Study." In A. Verbovsek, B. Backes, and C. Jones, eds., *Methodik und Didaktik in der Ägyptologie*. Ägyptologie und Kulturwissenschaft, 4. Munich: Wilhelm Fink Verlag, 313–326.

Hornung, E. 1989. *Die Unterweltsbücher der Ägypter*, 3rd ed. Zürich/Munich: Artemis Verlag. 140–151.

Hornung, E. 1999. *The Ancient Egyptian Books of the Afterlife*. Ithaca, NY: Cornell University Press.

Michalowski, P. 2010. "Traveler's Tales: Observations on Musical Mobility in Mesopotamia and Beyond." In R. Dumbrill and I. Finkel, eds., *ICONEA 2008: Proceedings of the International Conference of Near Eastern Archaeomusicology Held at the British Museum, December 4, 5, and 6, 2008*. London: ICONEA, 117–125.

Pearl, O. M., and Winnington-Ingram, R. P. 1965. "A Michigan Papyrus with Musical Notation." *Journal of Egyptian Archaeology* 51:179–195.

Pöhlmann, E., and West, M. L. 2001. *Documents of Ancient Greek Music: The Extant Melodies and Fragments*. Oxford: Clarendon Press.

Schafer, R. M. 1993. *The Soundscape*. New York: Destiny Books.

Sears, R. 2012. "The Practical Muse: Reconstructing the Contexts of a Greek Musical Papyrus." Ann Arbor: University of Michigan. Ph.D. dissertation.

Smith, M. 2009. *Traversing Eternity: Texts for the Afterlife from Ptolemaic and Roman Egypt.* Oxford: Oxford University Press.

Toop, D. 2010. *Sinister Resonance: The Mediumship of the Listener.* New York: Continuum.

Wiebach-Koepke, S. 2003. "Sehen und Hören in den Schilderungen der ägyptischen Unterwelt des Neuen Reiches." In N. Kloth, K. Martin, and E. Pardey, eds., *Es werd niedergelegt als Schriftstück: Festschrift für Hartwig Altenmüller zum 65. Geburtstag.* Studien zur altägyptischen Kultur Beiheft, 9. Hamburg: Helmut Buske Verlag, 477–489.

Wilfong, T. G. 2002. "'Friendship and Physical Desire': The Discourse of Female Homoeroticism in Fifth Century CE Egypt." In N. S. Rabinoitz and L. Auanger, eds., *Among Women: from the Homosocial to the Homoerotic in the Ancient World.* Austin, TX: University of Texas Press, 304–329.

Listening to Karanis: The *Mer-Wer Remix Project*

John Kannenberg

When I travel, I listen. I collect sounds the way other people collect pictures, by making field recordings of the sounds that surround me.

My artistic practice involves listening to spaces and places, particularly museums. To me, the auditory ambience within a museum contains a mix of historical and contemporary sounds, even if the aging objects in the museum are themselves mute. If sound really is an object (as the 20th-century composer and acoustician Pierre Schaeffer suggested) and if there truly is no such thing as silence (as John Cage discovered after his famous, if somewhat apocryphal, trip to a "perfectly silent" anechoic chamber), then the contemporary sonic experience of a museum can be said to be filled with historic and contemporary objects resonating with each other. Just as museum theorists describe the aura surrounding authentic objects as one of the factors that help give museums their value as sites of unique experiences, I like to describe the sonic environment within museums as *the active sounds of history*. Within these curated spaces filled with artifacts from other times, museum visitors are able to walk through time in an intersection of contemporary actions and historical objects that blends present and past, generating resonances between time periods that are able to be heard and in turn collected through the process of field recording.

So what does this have to do with Karanis?

In the summer of 2010, my interest in the sonic relationships between museums and ancient objects brought me to Egypt for the first time. I was on a research trip, a sound-collecting expedition. My primary hunting ground was the Egyptian Museum in Cairo, where I spent an entire week recording sounds that would later become the source material for a composition, a "sound map" that leads the listener on a museum audio tour of a different kind. But if I was interested in what museums sound like, traveling to the Egypt *outside* of its museums was a veritable goldmine: the entire country is a giant palimpsest, filled with ancient sites intersecting with the country's vibrant contemporary culture—ancient sites that act like artifacts within a giant collection curated by the Egyptian people through the ages.

Fig. 60. The Birket Qarun (Kelsey Museum neg. no. 5.2989).

I planned trips to as many ancient sites as possible in my time there, and a day trip to the western oasis of the Fayum—and Karanis—was high on my list.

Most of my day at Karanis was spent making recordings in the two ancient temples there while in the company of a local archaeologist from the Supreme Council of Antiquities along with several military personnel assigned to guard this somewhat remote site. The guards there were unsure what to make of my (more than slightly) strange behavior involving pointing microphones inside altar niches and standing still inside silent stone spaces. In fact, they became so suspicious they called for backup: while I stood at the altar of the Northern Temple with a microphone in my outstretched hand, a military helicopter emerged over the horizon and buzzed low, circling over my head before determining that whatever I was doing—while no doubt bizarre—wasn't threatening the ancient site. This unfortunately shattered the idealized "ancient silence" I had naively hoped to capture on tape; instead, I ended up collecting one of the most awesome helicopter recordings I will probably ever make.

My guide from the Supreme Council of Antiquities then took me to another location in the Fayum on my list of sonic "targets." The Birket Qarun (fig. 60; ancient name "Mer-Wer" or "The Great Lake") is a lake in the Fayum that, according to several ancient Egyptian creation myths, was the body of water from which all life originated—a real-life mythical lake of creation.

I wanted to make a hydrophonic (underwater) recording of the sound of the Qarun, although I was a novice at this and only had a simple, homemade hydrophone

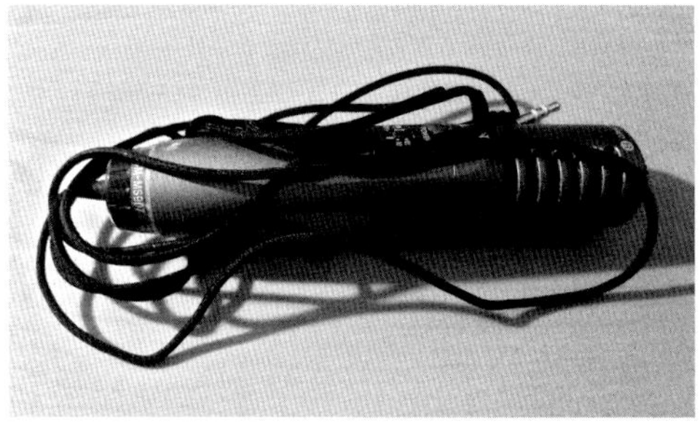

Fig. 61. Drowned microphone used for the Mer-Wer recordings (photo author).

to use. When I reached the Qarun, I was confronted by a steep slope of boulders on the edge of the lake, down which it was necessary to amble in order to get close enough to place the microphone in the water. Omar, the driver I'd hired for the day, enthusiastically volunteered to do it for me—but with my Arabic skills almost nonexistent, I was unable to communicate how fragile my microphone was. As I watched in horror, my makeshift hydrophone was fully submerged, banging relentlessly against the rocks on the shore. With a ruined, drowned microphone and what I assumed was a terrible recording in my possession, we made our way back to Cairo.

When I finally worked up the nerve to listen to Omar's recording a few days later, I was amazed: the impacts on the rocks, the gurgling water, and the plaintive squawks of failing electronics combined to create an experience of unexpectedly cacophonous beauty. Instead of disappointing, I found this recording captivating.

I immediately envisioned it as the focal point of an online remix project. Omar's recording would be offered as a free downloadable mp3 file on the Internet to anyone interested in using it as a sound source from which to make a piece of music. In turn, I would share the musical results that were submitted back to me on the same website, publishing successive "waves" of multiple pieces of drowned microphone music.

The project launched on the Internet in November of 2010, and there have been several waves of music files published since. My dead microphone, drowned in the mythical Great Lake, has found new life in an ongoing process of musical creation (fig. 61).

The Mer-Wer Remix Project *can be found at http://www.stasisfield.com/space/mer-wer. If you are interested in remixing the original recording, you can find instructions at the site for submitting your work.*

Acknowledgments

Both the exhibition "Karanis Revealed" and the present publication were the result of hard work and collective effort by the Kelsey Museum community. The exhibition appeared under Sharon Herbert's directorship of the museum and the publication under Christopher Ratté's directorship: I'd like to thank both for their support and encouragement. The exhibition was designed, prepared, and constructed by Museum Exhibition Coordinator Scott Meier, whose creativity has also influenced this publication. Former Kelsey Conservator Claudia Chemello conserved the majority of the exhibition artifacts and supervised their installation, while Kelsey Museum Associate Curator of Conservation Suzanne Davis and Kress Conservation Fellow Carrie Roberts carried out additional artifact conservation. Museum Administrative Specialist Carl Abrego and Museum Secretary Sandra Malveaux gave essential logistical support for both exhibition and publication. Former Associate Director Laurie Talalay and former Community Outreach Supervisor Todd Gerring gave outreach support, and thanks to Marlene Goldsmith for her tireless promotion via social media. Curator Elaine Gazda provided useful background and help from her own experience of exhibiting Karanis materials.

Thanks to Robin Meador-Woodruff, former Museum Registrar and Curator of Photographs and Slides, who introduced me to the Karanis archives and drew my attention to a number of the artifacts and images that appear in this publication. Thanks to Museum Graphic Artist Lorene Sterner for her meticulous line drawings for exhibition graphics and publication illustrations, and thanks to Michelle Fontenot, Collections Manager, for helping with access to collections and for arranging loans of papyri.

Special thanks are due to Sebastián Encina, Coordinator of Museum Collections, who helped with archival and artifact photographs and documents, as well as access to collections and new photography. Kelsey Museum Editor Peg Lourie copyedited, designed, and formatted text and graphics for the exhibition, as well as the present publication, with her usual taste and style, and I also want to thank her for her patience at my last-minute additions. My curatorial assistant Andrew

Ferrara was integral to object and image choice, case mockup, label and panel writing, image and text management, research and promotion for the exhibition, and essential to the planning and execution of this volume. Throughout the often fraught processes of exhibition and publication, Andrew was a constant source of expertise, hard work, enthusiasm, and good cheer.

The University of Michigan Library Papyrology Collection provided loans of papyri and related support, and I'd like to thank Adam Hyatt, James Cook, Nikos Litinas, Arthur Verhoogt, Shannon Zachary, and Brendan Haug for their help. Special thanks to Leyla Lau-Lamb for conservation work on papyri and for training Andrew Ferrara and myself in papyrus conservation (Andrew's work can be seen in the images for artifacts 74 and 124). Randal Stegmeyer, Library Photographer, contributed images of papyri and Kelsey Museum artifacts.

To the contributors to this volume—Claudia Chemello, Graham Claytor, James Cook, Sebastián Encina, Andrew Ferrara, Jen Gates-Foster, Adam Hyatt, John Kannenberg, Tom Landvatter, Rebecca Sears, and Drew Wilburn—I owe thanks for their contributions and for their patience through the publication process. I'd also like to thank John Kannenberg for the use of his *Mer-Wer Remix Project* graphic as a motif for both exhibition and publication cover, and for his sound installation in the exhibition.

As always, my friends have been a core source of encouragement and support in exhibition preparation and writing. In addition to those named above, I'd like to thank Chris Hinson, Greg Madden, Chet McLeskey, Carl Nyman, Janet Richards, and Gina Soter for keeping me going during the long processes of exhibition preparation and publication.

Finally, both exhibition and publication are dedicated to the memory of my late friend Traianos Gagos, who died in April 2010 just as preparation for "Karanis Revealed, Part I" was getting under way. Most of the people involved with "Karanis Revealed" were Traianos's friends, colleagues, and students, and even the few who never met him have become honorary "friends of Traianos" by association. Traianos and I spent many happy hours over beers across nearly two decades discussing and arguing about the Michigan Karanis material in our respective collections. The present volume appears four years after Traianos's death, but I still miss his friendship and wisdom every day.

T. G. Wilfong

Indices

Numbers in **bold** refer to artifact numbers in the catalogue, pp. 45–120; otherwise references are to page number.

Kelsey Museum Accession Numbers

University of Michigan Library Ostrakon and Papyrus Inventory Numbers

Expedition Field Numbers for Artifacts

(see explanation for numbering systems on p. 23)

Karanis Structure and Area Designations

Kelsey Museum Negative Numbers

General Subject Index